Who Cares?

The Profound History of Liability Law

Nelson P. Miller

Who cares? The profound history of liability law.

Miller, Nelson P.

Published by:

Crown Management, LLC
1527 Pineridge Drive
Grand Haven, MI 49417
USA

ISBN: 978-0-9905553-5-3

In the Perfect Person's honor.

Table of Contents

Dedication

The author dedicates this book to the everyday practitioners of the law of civil liability, to those persevering, patient, thoughtful, sensitive, just, and courageous men and women who hear, discern, evaluate, advocate, defend, and resolve the claims of the injured. The author particularly recognizes the work of these fellow members of that fine bar, Doug Allen, Tom Behm, Bob Blaske, Tom Blaske, Carole Bos, John Bredell, Judy Bregman, Rob Buchanan, Carol Carlson, Peter Davis, Steve Drew, Jim Fajen, Bill Farr, Brad Glazier, Bill Jack, Kevin Lesperance, Bob McCoy, Brian McKeen, Bill Mills Sr., Pat Nolan, Bud Roegge, Skip Pylman, Dave Shafer, Dale Sprik, Gary Stek, Jim Straub, and Matt Yokom.

Caring for the Law of Love

Law concerning itself so much with love, or more prosaically with *care*, might surprise some. Do lawyers truly care about care, care about love? *Tort law* is the misnomer with which law mislabels law's civil care. Lawyers may be too embarrassed to call it what it is. The word *tort* derives either from the Latin *tortus* meaning *twisted* or from the French word for *injured*. In that respect, the label may once have fit. Tort law's justification is certainly that something inappropriately twisted (a wrong) occasionally occurs resulting in injury that law intends to remedy. The trouble is that no one remembers what *tort* means, that wrongs occur needing righting. Instead, we misconceive profound law of care as tort law, indeed as annoying *liability* law, and thus widely disparage it.

Right now, tort law has an unusual need for both perspective and stability. Over the past couple of decades, the law of care has faced marked upheaval. To some, tort law is its own train wreck. As recently as 40 years ago, tort law had none of its present political attention, special-interest lobbying, propaganda advertising, judicial reversals and flip-flops, and piecemeal legislation. Then, the public accepted tort law as relatively stable and settled. Today, tort law is a political, legislative, and judicial hot potato. No one seems to know exactly, or even generally, what to do with tort law other than to criticize it.

1

Lawyers, judges, and law professors share blame for this fundamental confusion on as fundamental of an issue as care — as tort law. Law professors may not know, much less teach, tort law's remarkably ancient history. Law school casebooks teach tort law as if it were a recent invention when it is indisputably not. Law has included negligence and other civil-liability provisions since ancient times. Today, the dominant social evolutionists, legal realists, and pragmatic materialists see little or nothing of value in the profundity of the ancients. Materialism regards as spurious any concept so fundamental as *care* or, for that matter, justice, fairness, right or wrong, and good or evil.

Thus the leading law writer of our day suggests (hard to tell whether tongue in cheek) that the rich ought to be permitted to drive faster through the neighborhoods of the poor, notwithstanding the increased safety risk, because on an economic, materialist's model the time of the rich is worth more than the lives of the poor. Is this kind of speculation simply too farfetched to be of interest? Perhaps not: Justice Oliver Wendell Holmes, a father of modern materialist law, was a proponent of the forced sterilization of criminals and the "retarded," reflective of the social eugenics with which the country experimented early in the last century. With materialism dominant in the culture, the law expressly rejects and then insulates itself from foundational concepts like care.

And then we have political appeals to special interests, for which history and philosophy should be, but with the dominance of materialism are not, antidotes. Appeals to special interests, indeed appeals to self-interest, challenge tort law, which has as its foundation the brotherly or *care* form of love, all about consideration for one another. Tort law makes an easy political target when politics depends on appeals to self-interest. Those appeals undermine tort law at its foundation. The suave trial lawyers who are the public face of tort law make even easier targets than tort law, even though tort law's administration depends just as much on the buttoned-down insurance-defense counsel and responsible insurance claim representatives as it does on those easy-target trial lawyers. When few of us appreciate tort law's grand history and fundamental role, and when the culture

2

lacks a strong normative base, political attacks appealing to special interests and self-interest simply wither tort law.

Yet no matter the sources and causes of tort law's challenges and (year-after-year it seems) its imminent demise, why should we care about tort law? With two reasons even the devoted materialist might agree. One is that non-material concepts like *care* continue to have enormous significance. By recognizing such allegedly spurious concepts as care, we fundamentally change our material universe, indeed change it in a way that devotion to material principles never could. A normative pursuit and experience creates a materiality of certain kind that the materialist pursuit seldom does. Care changes our world.

Another reason to care about care (about tort law!) is that care, not the material pursuit of things, is the intrinsic activity of value. In an unavoidable way, human life has a distinct value beyond material comprehension. Care is the intrinsic good that recognizes that profound value. When we reject care in favor of material thinking and pursuits, we reject the humanity that care ennobles. And that rejection is not attractive. Once the materialist decides that we have only the material (in itself an unparalleled leap of non-material imagination), then human life becomes only a means or function related to whatever material end or design any individual chooses. When we reject care in favor of something allegedly more tangible (or at least allegedly more pragmatic), we give over our sensitivity for one another to an insatiably self-interested sensuality.

The law has not always been so materially minded, nor is it uniformly so today. The law has other strains, philosophies, and forms. Indeed the law has had a rich heritage of natural values and reason, although not much in vogue today. Immanuel Kant would have said that the categorical imperative — that which we must do above all else, by our very nature within the universe — is to always treat persons as ends and never means. For millennia the religious have said it more plainly that God is love. Yet no matter how one says it or whether one accepts it by tradition, personal experience, or logic, we easily reach the conclusion that care has no equivalent as an intrinsic good. All intrinsic goods including joy, peace, patience, and kindness are merely attributes of love.

We today fail to see that tort law is one form of this single most-fundamental value, obligation, and privilege to love. Tort law is formal, social, and governmental evidence of love, of the deep-rooted and sometimes self-sacrificial care that we owe one another, particularly around our personal well-being and integrity. Indeed more precisely, tort law is not so much the formal evidence of love but of our common willingness to recognize and address love's absence. Tort law is the palpable and measurable residue of love, identifying, judging, and redeeming the scum that remains when one empties the deep well of care. What we need — what the law needs, society needs, you and I need — is a long and rich view of this law of love.

~

To that end, Chapter 1 traces the ancient roots of the law of love. The conventional wisdom among law scholars is that the law recently invented care-based tort law (that is, fault-based tort law). Law students learn tort law in their first year of law school. Tort law is often a law student's first subject. The first words many law students read, from the classic and most-popular tort-law casebook's introduction, are that the English invented fault-based tort law to replace a primitive law of vengeance. Other tort texts follow the same lead down the wrong path. These historical assertions are factually false, even though supporting doctrinal and philosophical beliefs. Modern archaeology has shown that early laws include tort provisions, some so clear as to readily serve us in the same form today. Language, culture, and conventions shroud other ancient tort laws to varying degrees. Yet everywhere one looks, those ancient tort laws are present, for the most part not brutal or vengeful, or foolishly superstitious. Ancient societies had rather detailed and workable civil liability laws as an integral part of their justice systems.

Ancient tort laws are so common, similar to ours, and humane that one naturally wonders how they worked in ancient society.

4

To better understand legal history requires better understanding ancient societies. Thus Chapter 2 takes one ancient tort law, the Code of Hammurabi's admonition to the boatmen plying the Tigris and Euphrates Rivers that they must pay for any careless loss, and places it in the society and economy of the day. When we judge another age by our own experience, we are unlikely to understand their conventions. Every age seems so like and yet so unlike our own. The commerce of ancient Babylonia in which Hammurabi's careless boatman worked was both similar and dissimilar to commerce today. Babylonian geography, government, family structure, education, and commerce were like our own, yet Babylonians faced significantly different challenges and had significantly different ways of thinking about them and responding. To assume that careless Babylonian boatmen regarded their liability law with the same mixture of fear and anger that merchants today regard modern law would likely be only partially correct. And so consider how tort law worked in ancient Babylonia, the birthplace and cradle not only of law but of so much of civilization.

How then did ancient tort law span the ages? Although tort law began as mundane secular law, it was equally a part of the laws of the sacred Israelite nation. Tort law is essentially moral law. We cannot separate tort law from our conscience's core. Thus Chapter 3 shows that when Israel reiterated ancient Mesopotamian tort law, that law acquired a moral color having profound implications. Some sacred tort provisions, such as the Covenant Code's eye for an eye and tooth for a tooth, we must interpret with sensitivity to unique theological implications. Modern interpreters make the mistake of finding in those laws harshness, caprice, or superstition that the laws did not actually possess. Instead, the laws function subtly and profoundly, both then and now, morally and socially. The Israelites articulated their tort law in the following millennia. By the time of the Talmud's compilation, those laws were remarkably sophisticated, one could argue more so than our own, in distinguishing among degrees of responsibility. The Jews taught us that tort law does not simply regulate conduct between persons, after the fashion of the ancient Mesopotamians, but also reflect what we owe our creator.

We would indeed err by treating the love at the root of tort law as only an attribute to study, when love became a person, the incarnate deity who illustrated care in perfect human form while redeeming the careless into love's estate. With Christ's advent, tort law assumed new form. Canon law changed politics, governance, philosophy, science, and the course of human history, not to mention tort law, which thereafter explicitly required personal responsibility to a normative individual standard. Chapter 4 treats tort law's reasonably prudent person as the incarnate divinity. Why not treat the reasonable person with so much regard? Scholars find fashionable to denigrate the reasonably prudent person, indeed to urge that person's banishment from the law. Yet the reasonably prudent person has through ages proven a perfectly useful servant. The chapter's parable offers a fresh look at the reasonable person's qualities, both sublime and divine, in their curiously ordinary glory.

Today, we do not ground tort law in so solid a foundation as Christ's perfect demonstration of care and character. Ancient Mesopotamian and nearly ancient Middle Eastern tort law traditions also reached us by other spans. The Romans who conquered both regions brought with them their own tort laws while also subsuming tort laws they found among the populations they conquered. Rome's historic Twelve Tables included clearly demarked, readily intelligible, fault-based tort laws. The various institutes the Romans developed and adopted over the following centuries, such as those of Justinian, included substantially more detailed tort provisions. Some Roman torts seem so modern and familiar that one might assumes them a direct antecedent of today's tort law. The earliest European legal commentators whom we credit with having influenced modern laws were schooled in Roman law, while today none think of the Romans when considering tort law. Chapter 5 recaptures that lost Roman tradition.

History and divinity may be anathema to many contemporary law scholars. Law in modern secular states rests not on claims of divine authority or even on historical precedent. Law scholars nonetheless make supernatural and historical assumptions as leaps of their own secular form of faith, raising the question, how ought we to properly ground law, especially tort law? The hard-won Declaration of Independence, as social contract and authority for representative government, had clear ideas for the source of law. Its writers referred to a body of thought and law that we today call *natural law*, connoting not naturalism, realism, or materialism but rather the use of reason from which to draw principles to preserve and promote human well-being. America's founders and framers did not write especially of tort law, but natural-law scholars Hugo Grotius (a 17th-century Dutch playwright and jurist) and Samuel Pufendorf (Europe's first secular law professor) from whom the founders drew did address tort law. Grotius and Pufendorf each articulated the natural source and essential nature of tort law. Chapter 6 summarizes their writings as the modern natural and necessary basis for tort law.

Experience teaches us the exquisite quality of care, no matter care's history and source. Given care's centrality to tort law, one would think that law scholars might list and study care's attributes. As we exercise care in every one of the myriad of our endeavors, care must exhibit far more wondrous facets than any diamond. Yet few pay any attention to the qualities that care includes. Scholars who study tort law, indeed judges who instruct juries in care in cases involving tort claims, make only very short and inadequate reference to care's attributes. Strange indeed is our failure in scholarship and instruction because the many doctrines that tort lawyers use well illustrate care's attributes. Tort law discerns its rules and doctrines precisely to satisfy care's attributes. Thus Chapter 7 explores the attributes of care as would any modern reasoning scholar.

What sensitivity to the ages did we lose on the Beagle's keel? Charles Darwin never intended his theory of natural selection and evolution to apply to human social constructs. Yet evolutionary theory nonetheless took hold of the law and law schools. Scholar jettisoned law's past to accommodate new beliefs. Law students once studied Aristotle, the great Roman codes, and the scholasticism of Augustine and Aquinas, while developing their reason following the natural law of Grotius and Pufendorf. When Holmes and Langdell turned the law academy in the late 1800s to Darwinian ideology, they necessarily denigrated this richly useful and articulate past as primitive and even primordial, and not as they claimed in scientific pursuit but instead using a curiously mystic method and language. Chapter 8 illustrates these errors. It then describes what some more-sensitive contemporary scholars suggest to recover our rich legal history, on which to base more soundly our present tort law.

Chapter 9 then traces how tort law has changed in the past 100 years, as judges, lawyers, and policymakers changed how they justify and rationalize it. Tort law over the past 100 years lost its foundation. Scholars claimed that tort law's basis is both unknown and unknowable—even though care stood quietly ready to draw them to its foundation. Bereft of love's natural rationale, scholars turned to pragmatic, material, and economic models that disrespect not only care but also tort law itself and the lawyers who practice it. These models saw greater loss in a crushed tomato, and offered the tomato greater protection, than in the human lives and abodes poisoned by careless agents. The more controversial of these scholars traced economic and material models to natural ends, frankly and brutally regarding human life as of little worth and human living as inappropriate, when measured against the utility of the commerce and other purported interests with which that life and living seemed to interfere.

Eventually, tort law's academic misconception reached a sort of nadir. Chapter 10 describes a series of difficult and disappointing decisions that resulted from such foundational error. No less than the U.S. Supreme Court in one tort case expressly elevated the individual pursuit of a depraved intentional harm to the exalted state of an intrinsic good. In doing so, the Court bent the tender knee of care to bow before its greater god of individual expressive liberty, in a case in which the defendant admitted exercising that liberty with the purpose of destroying another. The Court continued to decide tort cases down that slippery slope until (in the words of one of its own members) it reached that slope's bottom in a decision protecting a savage sort of lawlessness.

How far can a society go in leaving behind the law of care? Policymakers have experimented at abolishing entirely the civil liability laws that reflect our fundamental duty of care to one another. While some of those measures were only at the state level and only in relatively narrow areas, New Zealand is one developed nation that tried the experiment broadly across all areas and at the national level. By and large, these experiments have failed to bring about the efficiencies that they sought to accomplish. What they did accomplish, studies show, is to place the burden of carelessness squarely on its innocent victims, indeed not alone on the injured but also on their spouses and children. Yet proposals to abolish tort law continue. The final Chapter 11 surveys these laws without care.

Consider one final note before embarking on this journey in care of care. We need not wring hands over threats to care, in the nature of criers predicting the fall of Rome. Care will most certainly survive without this or any other writing to help it. We all know deep down and intuitively that care wins, having a timeless dimension that its absence and opposite so sorely lack. This writing is simply a guidepost for those who wish to travel the ancient road of care, trusting in its sure direction and footing. You need only stand at the crossroads looking for that ancient path and, when you see it, to follow it resolutely—although you could further serve as sentinel for others. Care will always be with us. Indeed it measures our souls rather than we taking stock of it. The sentinel survives as long as executing the sentinel's duties. Where do you go?

Chapter 1

An Ancient Custom

Understand first the challenge of tracing tort law back to its origins. Tort law is for the most part *common law,* meaning an ever-changing body of relatively informal rules that accrete over the ages from individual decisions in particular cases. Surprising as it may seem, academics offer us no comprehensive bibliography for common law's source. We cannot go to the book shelf and pull down a volume to trace the common law back through the ages.

Oh, scholars do offer us well-known (if hoary) treatises like Pollock and Maitland's *History of English Law* and other works whose titles suggest a comprehensive treatment of the whole subject. We also find available excellent summaries of the common law's major influences such as Shaffern's *Law and Justice from Antiquity to Enlightenment.* Yet these texts are nothing like full bibliographies. They treat only periods or forms of the common law, and influences shaping it. One must instead fumble through catalogues containing (in one legal historian's words) yawning gaps that those interested in law can only barely attempt to fill. What then follows here is a partial but helpful survey of ancient tort rules reflecting principles similar to those appearing in our modern-day common law.

One might think that a good starting point for ancient law would be the great Code of Hammurabi, an inspiring inscription preserved on a seven-foot-tall inscribed dark-basalt stele in the Louvre and multiple clay tablets. Or possibly Moses' venerable Covenant Code would be the place to start. Both of these celebrated codes have tort provisions. Yet it now appears that both belonged in respects to a common law tradition throughout the ancient Middle East region in which they originated. Several similar ancient Sumerian laws, including word-for-word equivalents, predated both great codes. The region where archaeologists discovered these earliest Sumerian laws is that of modern-day Iraq, which was ancient Sumer, the Akkad, Mesopotamia, and Babylon. The writings were in cuneiform script, meaning wedge shapes pressed into clay tablets. The laws impressed on the oldest of these recovered cuneiform tablets were only fragments of larger law collections or codes. The earliest of these fragmentary laws scholars have come to know as the Laws of Ur-Nammu and Code of Lipit-Ishtar. The Laws of Ur-Nammu date to 2100 B.C., so about 4,100 years ago.

Both of the Laws of Ur-Nammu and Code of Lipit-Ishtar, like the later Code of Hammurabi and Covenant Code, include tort provisions. The tort provision that appears in the fragmentary Laws of Ur-Nammu states, "If a man knocks out the eye of another man, he shall weigh out 1/2 a mina of silver." Over four thousand years ago, at the dawn of recorded time, man was compensating man with money, for injury. With the public disdain that we show for modern civil-liability laws today, as if they are the new product of a modern society whose former self-responsibility has suddenly run amok, one almost has to stop to let the thought sink in. The very earliest law, in the very earliest form of writing, in the very earliest civilization capable of such writing, already included a civil-liability law. One who injures must pay for the injury.

Absent from this fragmentary law is any direct statement that the payment should go to the injured party. We might safely assume that the ancient law's intent was that the injurer pay the injured, though the law's sheer antiquity cautions against assuming anything. Also absent from this fragmentary law is any direct suggestion that fault was necessary to establish civil liability. The provision may instead have been what we know today as a *strict-liability* provision: if you injure, then you pay, with no showing of carelessness or negligence required. The injurer may not have been at all careless. Pure accident may have

11

caused the injured's lost eye. Thus this earliest law may not have expressed a fully developed rule of care. The prospect that one must pay for injury certainly implies a rule of care not to cause that loss, but the ancient rule may have been even broader than strictly a duty of care because it would appear to have included payment for purely accidental (non-negligent) injury.

Yet we find expressed in the other law of the same period, the Code of Lipit-Ishtar, precisely the duty of care that the Laws of Ur-Nammu only imply. The fragmentary Code of Lipit-Ishtar dates to circa 1930 B.C., so while also nearly 4,000 years old about 170 years newer than the Laws of Ur-Nammu. The Code of Lipit-Ishtar also had a tort rule. That fact would in itself bolster the view that ancient law was (like our law today) at least in part a law of care, indeed of that other-regarding love. Yet the Code of Lipit-Ishtar has just what the Laws of Ur-Nammu implied but failed to express: both a specific admonition that the injurer must pay the injured party plus a clear negligence rule within the broader rule for compensating for injury. The fragment of the Code of Lipit-Ishtar that survives addresses property loss rather than personal injury, but that property loss provision holds the careless one liable to pay damages to the owner of the property lost due to negligence:

§5: If adjacent to the house of a man the bare ground of another man has been neglected and the owner of the house has said to the owner of the bare ground, "Because your ground has been neglected someone may break into my house: strengthen your house," and this agreement has been confirmed by him, the owner of the bare ground shall restore to the owner of the house any of his property that is lost.

To see such care reflected in the very most-ancient laws that we are able to unearth and understand should astonish us. Where is the primitive, careless culture if not in our very oldest laws? We can only speculate whether even earlier, pre-literate cultures had similar laws requiring care toward one another. Yet on this extraordinary record, we would certainly do worse to conclude that earlier societies lacked those laws of care. From this evidence of the earliest of written laws including a civil-liability provision, the distinct probability arises that civil-liability laws existed even before the invention of writing. Why would such laws coincidentally arise with writing? No clear reason suggests why they would do so.

One might conjecture that these fragmentary civil-liability laws were peculiar even to their own culture and day. While we know that these ancient societies had civil-liability laws for the loss of eyes, maybe they did not have the same laws for the loss of life or limb. While these ancient societies had civil-liability laws for the neglect of ground, maybe they did not have civil-liability laws for the neglect of building, water, or cattle. Yet the earliest comprehensive code we have so far discovered, the Laws of Eshnunna, teaches us just the opposite, that comprehensive civil-liability laws were a part of ancient governance and culture.

Archaeologists discovered the Laws of Eshnunna in 1945 and 1947 in a Baghdad suburb. Ancient rulers wrote the Laws millennia earlier for the kingdom city of Eshnunna, located along a tributary to the east of the Tigris River. Scholars have not yet fixed precisely the time of their writing but believe them to be from no later than the 18th century B.C., which would mean at least 3,700 years ago. That dating would make the Laws of Eshnunna only a couple hundred years more recent than the fragmentary laws of Ur-Nammu and Lipit-Ishtar. Eshnunna's rulers wrote the Laws in the Akkadian language, which was a Semitic language of ancient Mesopotamia. The Laws of Eshnunna are the earliest collection of laws found in that language. (The earlier fragmentary laws were in the still-more ancient Sumerian language.)

The Laws of Eshnunna actually include *four* groups of tort laws. One group covers the handling of oxen, not a specific area of concern for modern tort law but a highly significant subject to that ancient economy. We should expect at least a few changes in the law of care between an early agrarian society and our own post-industrial information society. A second group of Eshnunna tort laws addressed building and maintaining sound walls of structures, while a third group addressed liability for biting dogs. Modern tort laws also address both of these areas of concern, buildings and biting dogs. One last grouping of Eshnunna tort laws had to do with the careless boatman. While modern tort laws, like the ancient Laws of Eshnunna, also address maritime accidents, we might take the ancient boatman laws as the equivalent of our motor-vehicle liability laws, given the significance of river travel to the ancient society.

When we look more closely at the Laws of Eshnunna, they appear broadly representative of tort rules today. Take for example the first group having to do with the goring ox, a theme common to ancient law practice. Indeed, ancient goring-ox rules are so common that scholars debate whether to attribute their similarity to their having a single source or merely such obvious efficacy. In either case, Eshnunna's goring-ox rules addressed several different eventualities. The Laws' first goring-ox rule had the owners of the goring and dead ox divide both living and dead ox as a remedy, somewhat like Solomon's splitting-the-baby wisdom. A rule to divide a living ox does not necessarily mean the ox's death. The rule instead gives the claimant the leverage to negotiate a settlement with the goring ox's owner to spare the goring ox. Eshnunna's divide-the-goring-ox rule did not require fault on the part of the goring ox's owner. Rather, the rule appears to have been one for strict liability. Yet the Laws' next goring-ox rule was a fault-based tort rule requiring the owner's knowledge of the ox's goring propensity and failure to guard against it:

> If an ox [was] a gorer and the ward [authorities] have had it made known to its owner, but he did not guard his ox and it gored a man and caused him to die, the owner of the ox shall weigh out 2/3 of a mina of silver.

Eshnunna also based its remaining tort laws on fault. Its dog-bite law provided:

> If a dog [was] vicious and the ward [authorities] have had [it] made known to its owner, but he did not guard his dog and it bit a man and caused him to die, the owner of the dog shall weigh out 2/3 of a mina of silver.

The owner first had to know of the dog's vicious propensities and then fail to guard against those propensities before the owner would be liable for the dog's wrong. The provision approximates modern common-law one-free-bite dog-bite rules, although modern statutes often provide for strict liability. Eshnunna had a similar, fault-based rule for a collapsing decrepit wall, that the wall's owner paid money for resulting damage, provided first that the wall was unsuitably decrepit and its owner therefore on notice of its need for repair, again like one might expect of modern rules.

The Eshnunna careless-boatman provision was even clearer than the above dog and wall civil-liability laws: "If a boatman was negligent and caused the boat to sink — as much as he caused to sink, he shall pay in full." The key word *negligent* was of course in the ancient Akkadian, its pronunciation unknown because the language long ago became extinct. Yet scholars in the Akkadian language define this fault concept equivalent to *negligence* and *carelessness*. In reading this ancient law consistent with our modern negligence law, we are not injecting our own modern concept. Fault, negligence, or carelessness was an attribute well known to Eshnunna citizens and thus operative in their civil-liability law. The other early laws may simply cite specific negligence examples without explicitly generalizing a modern negligence concept, but the careless-boatman provision clearly stated a general rather than specific conduct rule, establishing an objective, external standard for conduct. Its damage provision was equally modern: payment commensurate with the full value of the damage.

Scholars have also noticed that Eshnunna's civil-liability laws illustrate situations of increasing gravity, from ox goring ox, to dog biting human, collapsing wall, and finally careless boatman, the rules thus providing further order behind the chaos that they govern. They also address both commercial and personal circumstances, property and services, and productive and unproductive activities, approximating our modern laws not only of negligence but of construction defects, products liability, and malpractice. Yet notwithstanding their clarity, generality, and relative comprehensiveness, Eshnunna's civil-liability laws merely foreshadowed the greater laws that soon followed.

Archaeologists discovered the Code of Hammurabi in excavations in Susa in southwestern Iran just at the turn of the last century. Scholars translated and published its inscriptions in 1902. Rulers wrote the Code for Hammurabi's ancient Babylonian kingdom. Conquerors brought the grand copy discovered at Susa from Babylonia to Elam as spoils of war, erasing part of it to provide for a victory inscription. Scholars date the Code to no later than the early 17th century B.C., making the Code about 3,600 years old and about a century more recent than the Laws of Eshnunna. Hammurabi's Code, like the Laws of Eshnunna written in the Akkadian language, far outlived the Sumerian laws from Ur-Nammu and Lipit-Ishtar and the Akkadian Laws of Eshnunna. Assyrian kings were still copying Hammurabi's Code in the 7th century B.C., a millennium later.

As in the case of the even-earlier civil-liability laws, we should be cautious when interpreting Hammurabi's ancient Code. The Mesopotamians living under its rules viewed the world differently than we do. They were polytheistic, imagining their world influenced by an infinite number of independent forces defying classification. We by contrast perceive universal design in cause, force, and effect, captured in elegant mathematical equation. It would not aid our inquiry to regard the Mesopotamians as primitive. Our age may hold its own error, perhaps in godless elevation of ourselves over everything, a modern presumption in which Hammurabi's subjects would definitely not have participated. They knew too readily their subject status, even if they attributed it too readily to many gods' whims. Modern materialists too firmly deny supernatural order, while Hammurabi's subjects were too ready to find the supernatural in everything.

Nonetheless, the Code does have an extraordinarily rational structure, composed of broad and then subsidiary themes, addressing ordered subgroups of subjects through normative rules. Each subgroup first states rates for the actor to charge for the particular agricultural or other economic activity under consideration. Each subgroup then gives examples of wrongful conduct that might occur in the actor's performance, then identifying the liability to attached to the wrong, often employing what we still today employ, which is a framework of culpable negligence. The Code's astonishing life-span may well have been

16

due to its soundly rational structure around a perfectly natural law of care. No wonder it long survived.

These specific tort-liability subsections of Hammurabi's Code first address the builder whose negligent construction of a home causes wrongful death or other damage. The Code then proceeds to rules addressing negligent construction and navigation of a boat, for instance requiring compensation for loss of the boat and cargo when a river pilot violates river-traffic right-of-way rules. Modern law uses a driver's violation of motor-vehicle traffic-safety codes in the same way as a presumption of negligence for which the driver will owe compensation for resultant harm. The Code's next rules deal with the wrongful taking of an ox from its owner, as well as the liability of an ox's lessee for its injury or death while in the lessee's possession. The Code's ox series concludes with liability rules for wrongful death caused by a goring ox. Similar rules follow, dealing with other common aspects of economic activity of the day. The Code is in that respect comprehensive.

Scholars translated some of the clearer Hammurabi's Code fault-based civil-liability rules in 1904 shortly after their discovery as follows:

CH229: If a builder has built a house for a man, and his work is not strong, and if the house he has built falls in and kills the householder, that builder shall be slain.

CH232: If goods have been destroyed, he shall replace all that has been destroyed; and because the house that he built was not made strong, and it has fallen in, he shall restore the fallen house out of his own personal property.

CH235: If a boat-builder has built a boat for a man and his work is not firm, and in that same year that boat is disabled in use; then the boat-builder shall overhaul that boat, and strengthen it with his own material, and he shall return the strengthened boat to the boat-owner.

CH236: If a man has given his boat on hire to a boatman, and the boatman is careless, and the boat is sunk and lost; then the boatman shall replace the boat to the boat-owner.

CH 251/252: If a man's ox (was) a gorer and the ward (authorities) have had made known to him that (it was) a gorer, but he did not screen its horns, (or) did not tie up his ox and that ox gored a son of a man and caused him to die, he shall give ½ a mina of silver.

Notice that in CH 229 and CH 232 the work of building a house must be "strong," while in CH 235 the work of building a boat must be "firm," in CH 236 the guiding of a boat must not be "careless," and in CH 251/252 a known gorer must be screened or tied up. In each instance, violating the rule of care requires the violator to compensate for resulting harm. The Code contains a rich assortment of similar liability laws including for a combatant negligently striking a man causing injury (CH 206), a herdsman's fault causing a loss of sheep and cattle (CH 267), the flooding of a rented field causing a loss of the harvest (CH 45-46), and a man "too lazy" to fix his dykes (CH 53) or who negligently opens his irrigation ditches causing a neighbor's loss of crops (CH 55).

Hammurabi's Code did not restrict civil liability to fault. It also provided strict liability for loss in the course of several kinds of bailment (see CH 242-249, 263, 266-267), as modern law also does in some instances, vehicle-owner consent statutes being a prime example. Yet the Code made fault-based rules the common and fundamental remedy, occasionally specifying specific standards of care around that fundamental duty. For example, the Code's goring ox rules include not merely the failure to guard the ox but also enumerate two alternative means of guarding, (1) to screen the ox's horns or (2) to tie up the ox. These two examples impress upon the modern reader that the ancient writer intended that the keeper base care of the ox on an external, community-based standard, just as modern law would require. Norms compelled then, as they compel today, that actors exercise ordinary care to prevent the harm. Hammurabi's Code was equally clear in stating the consequence of breaching that duty, that the actor pay money to compensate for the harm. So much like modern tort law, the ancients treated private loss in quantitative, qualitative, and objective terms, permitting a pecuniary recovery precisely where doing so seemed most just. The modern reader would find it no more difficult to generalize a maritime negligence law from the Code's boat rules, and other standards of care for other activities. Tort concepts of negligence, notice, knowledge, objective standards for conduct, and monetary compensation for harm did not await modernity, no less Renaissance dawn. Ancients knew their tort law.

Chapter 2

A Careless Boatman

Some years ago philologist Jacob Finkelstein published, although posthumously, an elegant monograph titled *The Goring Ox*, about the biblical laws holding ox owners civilly liable for injury and damage. Reacting to the social Darwinism of his day, the monograph's cautious author laid out the reasonable principle that we ought to know something of an ancient people before we judge their laws as primitive. Finkelstein used the biblical goring-ox rules to illustrate his principle.

Contrary to what the social Darwinists had supposed, Finkelstein's study of the language and cosmology of the people who wrote and followed those civil-liability laws suggested that the laws were quite sensitive in their conception, not merely for their time but for any time. Finkelstein did not attempt broader study of the geography, society, economy, and other important aspects of those ancient times. He limited his study to the peculiarities of the language and cosmology of the ancients whose goring-ox rules he wished to understand. Perhaps Finkelstein's extraordinary philological skill and sensitivity limited his study. His interests were language and mind. He could translate directly the ancient texts, knowing not only the ancient Hebrew but also the even more ancient Akkadian and Sumerian scripts. Yet he knew little of goring oxen and may have known not much more of the ox-men of the time.

While the goring-ox rules have been a favorite subject of scholars, scholars might better have studied the careless boatman. We should be more concerned with human than animal behavior.

The ox's unpredictability complicates consideration of the responsibility and legal liability of the ox's owner. Ancient laws regulating the careless boatman involve no such bovine complication. Both the Laws of Eshnunna and Hammurabi's Code, cited and quoted in the prior chapter, expressly condemn the boatman's carelessness while expressly creating civil liability for resulting loss. The ancient goring-ox rules require an inference (obvious to some, less obvious to others) that they refer to negligence. The boatman laws require no inferences. Their express use of the negligence concept makes them a better departure point to study ancient tort law than nebulous goring-ox rules. So consider in context the ancient boatman's negligence rules.

Of course, Babylon is long gone. Isaiah's prophecy of the once glorious Babylon's utter demise has certainly come true. Despite Saddam Hussein's modern ambition to restore Babylon's glory in order to place his own name alongside that of Nebuchadnezzar II, the site of Babylon remains little more than heaps of sterile earth sprinkled with fragments of brick. We must instead look to ancient records to learn of the Babylonian Society in which the ancient-boatman rules worked. Hammurabi's Code, written by the best Babylonian scholars of the day, is one source not only of the rules themselves but also of their commercial context insofar as the rules regulate specific services or trade of concern. Yet to appreciate more fully the careless boatman's civil-liability law, we ought to draw not only from the Code in which the law appears but also the hundreds of Babylonian business documents the British Royal Museum has preserved for study by scholars. None, however, have focused on the ancient tort laws.

Consider for example the waters that our careless boatman plied in the best way of moving goods in ancient Mesopotamia. Babylonia's Tigris and Euphrates Rivers (two of the four rivers flowing out of the Bible's Eden) together with their tributaries and many southern canals reached most of the region. The Tigris and Euphrates Rivers, roughly parallel while separated by from 40 to 90 miles, span from northwest to southeast a plain of hundreds of thousands of square miles. The Euphrates forms on a plateau at 11,000 feet above sea level, flowing southeast for 1,800 miles while

21

falling in elevation about one foot per mile during the last two thirds of its length. Small boats navigate the Euphrates from when its waters rise in March and flood in late May until late September. The Tigris is shorter at only 1,150 miles and begins at an elevation of only 5,000 feet, but its waters rise much earlier and may flood more rapidly and broadly than the Euphrates, covering miles in certain areas. Three well-known ancient cities Nineveh, Nimrood, and Asshur sat on the banks of the Tigris. Today, the Euphrates and Tigris Rivers join before flowing, as the Shatt al-Arab, their last 80 miles into the Persian Gulf. The cuneiform record suggests that in ancient times the Gulf reached 130 miles farther inland such that the rivers would not have joined when our careless boatman navigated them. Since ancient times, the rivers have become the Great Swamp before entering the Persian Gulf.

Consider then the surrounding geography, much like the better-known geography of Egypt, a dry and fairly desolate upper river region giving way to a rich lower delta. As in Egypt, society in general and the life of our careless boatman in particular would have depended entirely on the rivers, especially the wider, slower, and therefore more easily navigated and controlled Euphrates. The plain down which the Tigris and Euphrates Rivers run has two distinct regions known then as Assyria in the northwest and Babylon in the southeast. Together, these regions comprised what the ancients called *Mesopotamia* from the Greek meaning "between the rivers." The Assyrian plain is a hot-and-dry desert canvas of stones. Sheep forage for the rough seasonal vegetation in the absence of crops. In contrast, the Babylonian plain has rich river deposits covering as much as 14,000 square miles under cultivation in ancient times.

Important to the commerce of our careless boatman, the city of Babylon (as distinguished from the region) had its location about one third up the Euphrates River at a point closest to the Tigris, not far from the present city of Baghdad and central to the Mesopotamian region. The ancient Assyrian capitol Nineveh was north of Babylon nearer the headwaters of the Tigris. Civilization began on this rich plain. Our boatman's carelessness has peculiar historical relevance in both necessitating Hammurabi's civil-liability rule and also ensuring that Hammurabi created reliable evidence of that law. One can almost hear, in his civil-liability rule, Hammurabi wondering just what to do with those darn careless boatmen.

The extensive canals our ancient boatman plied, and the dykes by which he navigated, reflected the rivers' importance to the ancients. The early Sumerians began building dykes about three millennia before Christ to control the rivers' annual floods. They then carved canals to water the plain for cultivation of plentiful date palms, maize-like grain, and other crops. The canals supported substantial population and commerce increase. Boats navigated the larger canals, which were up to 130 yards wide with a bottom lined in stones and earthen banks strengthened at critical points with baked bricks set in bitumen — engineering marvels for an ancient people. The canal at Takrit was so large that the Tigris jumped its bed to flow for centuries through the canal's channel, long after our careless Babylonian boatman's demise. This extraordinary channel known in modern times as the Serpent River for its circuitous course had substantial ancient boat traffic.

The Euphrates regularly changed course along much of its length, making a gradual march westward. The great river's westward march required continuous rebuilding of cities and towns along its banks and on the banks of its streams and canals. Our careless boatman would have found substantial hazard in these constant changes as the river scoured, flooded, and silted. River-traffic hazards on North America's comparatively settled Mississippi River are popular literature and lore. Navigating the migrating Euphrates must have been far more hazardous. Ancient disputes under Hammurabi's civil-liability provision may well have included whether the boatman should have attempted voyage at certain times on certain waters to beat or avoid a flood, transport on a rising or falling current, and so forth. We should wonder whether the ancient disputants would have called experienced boatman as expert witnesses, as we surely would today.

The rivers and canals bore other substantial marks of design and habitation. Our ancient boatman navigated his craft along canals lined with brick set in a natural tar that we today call *bitumen*. Enormous baked-brick works lay at canal mouths to regulate water flow, their workers a common sight. Cities had their wharf district along the river or a primary canal, functioning not only for docking and mooring ships and boats but also for offices regulating trade and exchange rates. Babylonian cities had no other commercial center than that of the wharf. Indeed, the wharf district had some administrative independence offering protected status to citizens like our careless boatman and foreign traders storing shipments. Merchants showed permits to pass royal checkpoints along the Euphrates River, perhaps like drivers use electronic passes on today's toll roads.

The many cities, towns, and villages along the rivers and canals, and the extensive farming and commerce, generated heavy river traffic. Our boatman may have used one of the canal maps archaeologists have recovered, suggesting that his carelessness may have been due to unfamiliarity with the waterways. The view from Babylon river bank would have given glance of Persian Gulf ships unloading copper ingots, smaller boats unloading alum from far up the Euphrates River, and still smaller boats loading sesame to convey to a downstream temple city. Given the river trade's quantity, our careless boatman may have moored his boat safely away from crowded wharf docks while awaiting his turn to transfer cargo. His negligent failure to securely moor his boat may have caused his cargo loss. Activity along the river and canal banks, and a good number of official duties, may have distracted our careless boatman from navigation hazards.

Rivers were so significant to the Babylonians that they regarded them as sacred. Their legends of the great Flood are an example. Evidence suggests that those legends existed among the native inhabitants even before the first Sumerian settlers who when adopting them recorded them as indigenous. One legend spoke of a great flood of the Tigris and Euphrates Rivers in conjunction with a torrential downpour, an event which except for its extent would not have been unusual to the region, especially before the proliferation of the dyke and canal systems. The legends are noteworthy primarily for the moral lessons their keepers drew from them. They held the Flood as sent to destroy the corrupted king and other sinners, saving only the righteous man Uta-Napishtim whose ark, like Noah's, came to rest on a mountain. Our boatman would have prayed to the god Shamash for courage to overcome evil wind, whirlwind, and hurricane spirits interfering with river navigation. The rivers judged the living. Judgment by flood, trial by river ordeal, and the constant threat of perishing from natural river hazards would all have burdened our careless boatman who drew daily reminder from the unpredictable waters.

Boats, like rivers, had prominent place, even sacred status, in Babylonian culture, which held the earth itself to be an upside-down riverboat of the kind the rivers still carry today. Archaeologists find model boats in the region's ancient tombs, which depict gods on divine boat voyage. Nebuchadnezzar II recorded that a boat inlaid with precious stones carried a god image to Babylon's annual New Year festival. The legendary Uta-Napishtim built a great sailing ship as wide as long and coated with bitumen, to load with grain at the god Ea's command in order to survive the great Flood. Having survived the Flood with the great ship's help, Uta-Napishtim and his wife became immortal residents at the river mouth. Thus our careless boatman would have treated his vessel both as a common Babylonian object and sacred symbol, as some commercial drivers today treat their 18-wheelers, although perhaps not to the same sacred degree.

Two types of riverboat were common. The coracle or kuffah, still in use today, was an ingenious round basket of plaited rushes or willow, a surprise to the Europeans who first viewed it. Skins covered the coracle, the flat bottom of which bitumen caulked. Two to four crew members navigated the coracle, which could hold several men and horses at once. The more-conventional kelek was a reed raft of wood, unconventionally buoyed by inflated goatskins. Ancient drawings depict boatmen navigating keleks loaded with stone, bales, and timber cargo, using punting poles for guidance. The coracle was better in fast waters but the kelek was better in rapids and shallows. The kelek had the advantage of easy dismantling for caravan transport back up river. Boatmen also used canoes with paddles and larger timber barges, although few because of the scarcity of timber. Watercraft typically carried between 55 and 155 bushels of grain. Boat building was a large industry. Hammurabi's Code had no fewer than seven sections relating to boats including one to set the price for caulking and another providing a penalty for improper caulking.

To our point, though, our careless boatman faced different risks in operating either coracle basket or kelek raft, than boat pilots face today. Although peculiarly suited to the waterways and available materials and technologies, the ancient craft carried substantially greater risk of failure than watercraft constructed today. Our careless boatman faced far greater peril of loss from the nature of his vessel alone, not merely from the turbulent waters he navigated. He steered smaller boats by rudder. Larger and heavier boats, rafts, and barges he navigated with punting poles or by towing from the river bank. Sailing he found unproductive. Unlike in Egypt with its Nile River, Babylon's prevailing winds blew downstream, making upstream water travel extremely difficult and upstream land travel preferred. Upstream 60-mile tow would take 17 days but the same 60 miles of downstream poling just 4 days. When reaching downstream river end, boats transferred their cargos to ships that sailed into the Persian Gulf, the Red, Arabian, and Mediterranean Seas, and the Indian Ocean, and may have circumnavigated Africa. None of these propulsion means, not current, pole, tow, or sail, had the power of modern internal-combustion engine. Accordingly, our ancient boatman's hazard in overcoming wind and current to manage his vessel were substantially greater. On the other hand, the smaller size and slower speed of his vessel made for smaller losses even if more frequently realized.

These inferences help us appreciate Hammurabi's civil-liability law's effect. Yet we should also know enough about our ancient boatman to understand how he might have regarded a liability rule discouraging carelessness. Today, distinctive tells dot the Mesopotamian region, as evidence of millennia of intensive habitation, indeed history's first urban civilizations. Artifacts indicate that agricultural settlements populated the region in the late Stone Age around 5,000 B.C. The earliest inhabitants were Sumerians, then Semitic Babylonians and Assyrians. We know little from whence the Sumerians came, whether as warring desert nomads or Central Asian farmers driven from their own lands. Sumerians may have had the heritage of inhabitants of Northern India or other regions to the east or northeast. They may even have been native to the south until the Persian Gulf inundated those lands. Sumerians were metalworkers who readily displaced stone-weapon-bearing earlier native inhabitants of lower Babylon. Excavations at Ur from about 2,600 B.C. produced exquisite adorned harp, gold helmet, and metal dagger. Our careless boatman plied the waters of a true, even if ancient, civilization.

Later Semites who gradually displaced early Sumerians (the even-earlier Stone Age inhabitants were also probably Semites) were likely from the regions to the south and west including Arabia. Their ancient languages Akkadian and Aramaic are kin to Hebrew and Arabic in the modern tongue. An influx of Semitic Amorites, after the last great Sumerian dynasty about two millennia before Christ, established Semitic Babylonian dominance for the rest of antiquity. Mesopotamia's population at the time was around one million and growing. Not until the Persian conquest in 539 B.C. and Greek influence that followed would the Hammurabic way of life established well more than a millennium earlier finally wane. Babylonia then lay lost and largely forgotten, particularly after the rise of the Arabs in the region centuries after Christ. Babylonia's rediscovery, excavation of its ancient sites, and deciphering of its languages are nearly as interesting as Babylonia's demise. Although European travelers reached Mesopotamia as early as the 12th century B.C., European expeditions did not begin to collect archaeological evidence of Babylonia until the late 18th and early 19th century A.D. Deciphering of cuneiform texts did not bring ancient Babylonia to life until the latter half of the 19th century.

We know thus that our careless boatman worked in a society the forms, structure, and culture of which changed only gradually over a thousand years. The boatman regarded traditional practices including his civil-liability law as fixed, much in contrast to modern society's frenetic pace of change. Our boatman

27

expected to live for not much more than 40 years, hoping to die quietly of old age at home but with death by battle, flood, starvation, or infectious disease likelier. He had decent burial on his side curled up under a clay bowl or wrapped in a reed mat, unless of means then in a clay coffin under or alongside his home.

Our boatman enjoyed considerable freedom. Hammurabi's Code gave Babylonians classes of nobles, working citizenry living in special quarters in the cities and not owning lands, and absolute slaves branded and shaved of head. Class had flexible status. Freeman could become enslaved or slave freed. Ethnicity had little role in class status. Slaves did the hard work of building, clearing, and maintaining the canals plied by our careless boatman who was of the freeman class but dealt with slaves who owned property and engaged in business. Boatmen, one tenth of the population of river towns, owned male and female slaves for crews. Temples owned one eighth of the lands, with the rest in private, family, or clan hands. Our boatman shared and enjoyed the considerable private wealth in circulation with an ancient entrepreneur's freedom, Hammurabi's Code itself securing his base wages. Early Sumerians lived in reed-mat huts, while later Babylonians lived in huts or rectangular houses made of bricks on the lower courses with mud-brick superstructures. A simple house might have had a bed or couch for the husband even if not for the rest of the family, a small table, clay or metal cookware, clay bowls, jars, and lamps, reed mats, and a corn grinder. Dress was simple and varied with climate and class. Sandals and shoes were common. The climate and cleanliness conventions required frequent washing and changing. Our boatman gave too much attention to shaving and hairstyles, also using perfumes and facial cosmetics.

Our careless boatman ate a plentiful but mostly vegetable diet, using washed fingers to draw from common family tray or bowl. He drank from the rivers and canals, adding a little palm wine on special occasions and choosing from among several kinds of beer available at taverns. His carelessness sometimes arose in the course of his having been too long and too frequent at those taverns. Friends enticed him, according to ancient business documents making frequent use of the Sumerian word for companion.   Those friends included other boatmen and tradesmen such as carpenters, leather-workers, fishermen, potters, and masons.

Our boatman lived with and provided for his own family as part of morals that included that his adultery not break up his own or another family. Law treated adulterers harshly. Divorce, while stigmatized, was possible for adultery or childlessness. A divorced or separated wife had spousal support available only in later times.   An early Sumerian code predating Hammurabi prohibited son from dishonoring father or mother, and wife from hating husband and vice versa. Our boatman led his own house with all that mastery entailed including providing food and shelter for family from business income. His wife had her own substantial rights including spending, investing, and managing her dowry, and conveying property away on death. She lent money at interest, sued in her own name, and owned and managed business. She loaned a portion of her dowry to her boatman husband to operate his business on the condition that he return equitable profits. If our careless boatman used his wife's dowry to buy his boat, then ancient lore reports that he suffered his wife's wrath when his carelessness realized civil liability. These conventions contributed to the strength of Babylonian community and economy. While Mesopotamian women enjoyed the above rights and commonly held temple jobs including priestess, they only on rare occasions served as scribes, did not otherwise commonly work outside the home, and would not have piloted a river boat. Hence, boat*man* is fair usage despite its singular gender identity.

Our careless boatman desired and had children, preferring male children for their services and to carry family name. Monogamy was the norm, but if our boatman's wife bore no children, then our boatman had a second wife or concubine to fulfill that function, or he and wife adopted. Average families had two to four children survive early childhood. Infant mortality rates were high in part because of the preference for male children, no surprise to moderns accustomed to sex selection during and even (in some regions) after pregnancy, and high rates of abortion.   Dealing in children occurred, but children nonetheless played games with other children and even adults, on a clay board with bones and pebbles and with a little gambling. Upper-class boys and girls learned to read and write cuneiform in schools and colleges attached to the temples and, later on as the demand for scribes increased, in secular schools.

Schools used legal rules, contracts, and verdicts as teaching tools, versing scribes in law. Younger upper-class children walked from home to the tablet-house school each day where they copied tablets to learn by heart under a headmaster and also studied mathematics. Akkadian-speaking Babylonian students first learned in Sumerian, though instruction in Sumerian eventually lapsed. Homework followed tablet-house schoolwork. Boys consigned to learn a trade did so as soon as they could contribute. Young men married only with father's permission and then remained with their families for some years after marriage. Our careless boatman may thus have had a son or two with him in the boat, their youth, inexperience, or play contributing to the loss of cargo.

Our boatman accepted father, mother, and siblings as relatives in nuclear family. He expected to receive an inheritance by testament or will in favor of heir. Property rights vested in family units, similar to modern practice except for the absence of capital-accumulating private corporations. Our boatman's expectation of inheritance would have been strongest if he were the eldest son. His inheritance included not only a share of his father's gold, silver, furniture, and other personal property but also his father's home and offering table or shrine. These expectations bear on our study of the boatman's civil liability. Civil liability could certainly discourage, frustrate, and sometimes defeat accumulation of property, if tort creditors were able to seize the careless boatman's property in satisfaction of civil-liability judgment. Our boatman would thus have strongly desired to avoid carelessness, if only to amass and hold property sufficient to satisfy the needs and interests of his children for an inheritance. Just as importantly, merchants who shipped their cargoes with our boatman would have had the same concern and interest.

Indeed, Hammurabi's Code itself tells us much about our careless boatman's economy. He exchanged loose-silver money, although not coins, which would not appear until about 650 B.C. in what is now western Turkey. He also received payment in maize, wool clothing, wine, and oil. With payment, the boatman bought not only oxen, sheep, and donkeys but also servants. By the time of the first powerful Akkadian rulers of the region, caravan trade occurred with Syrians, Arabs, and Elamites. Quarries for gold, silver, copper, and marble were common, and the temples imported costly woods, all of which river barges carried. Paid labor received two-and-a-half gallons of barley plus rations of bread and beer as daily wage. Interest as high as 20 percent on loans of silver impoverished borrowers. Our boatman's carelessness may have been due to navigational shortcuts taken to avoid or pay debt. Accounting tracked income, expense, and debt. Wealth accumulated, especially after Persians invaded. The richer invested in notes and contracts based on silver standard. Family firms ran trade, capitalized in partnership and through individual and temple loans, advances, and investments. The commercial system was clearly sophisticated enough for merchants to demand and receive financial accountability from a careless boatman. The primary feature lacking was liability insurance.

Engineering was equally advanced. Babylon's Tower of Babel, on the Euphrates' east bank, rose to a height of 300 feet from 300-foot square base. A 300-foot bridge spanned the river to a large suburb on the opposite bank. Hazarding his navigation, our boatman gazed awestruck at other structures including Babylon's ten miles of huge double security walls, 20 feet thick and 40 feet apart, enabling chariots to defend the city's perimeter. Nimrud's huge quay wall on the Tigris provided access to its ziggurat, each stage of which builders had inlaid in a different color and priests had dedicated to Sun, Moon, or planets Saturn, Jupiter, Mars, Venus, and Mercury. Brick-lined moats encircled Babylon's great walls, our boatman's cargo gaining entrance only through 25-foot-wide towers every 150 feet. The city intimidated our boatman into treating circumspectly civil-liability and other laws, administrators of which were quite capable of holding him accountable. Silver or even gold plated the beams, doors, and roofs of city temples at the end of streets lined with glazed brick. These riches did not intimidate the Euphrates River, which changed its course, slowly contributing to Babylon's abandonment.

The region's major natural resources included only water, good soil for agriculture, and the asphalt-like bitumen seeping from the ground in the southern lake region. Imports provided stone, timber, and minerals. Labor and its administration, not abundant natural resources, drove the economy, which military victories alternately aided and disrupted. Successful repulse of invading marauders resulted in spoils, strengthening of city walls, enlargement of strategic cisterns, and development of further canals. Citizens of the most prominent cities raised their living standards with exemption from conscription and taxes. Trade on our boatman's vessels was the Mesopotamian economy's peculiar strength. Timber came from mountains to the northeast and west, metals from north and east, silver from northeast, gold from Egypt and India, and precious stones from north. Babylon thus owed its nearly five-thousand-year existence to its strategic location for trade from all four compass directions. Trade compelled Hammurabi to make Babylon his capital and enlarge and strengthen it. Donkey caravans were important, but the essential transport was our boatman's vessel bringing trade goods downriver to cities and towns, and exports to ships sailing into the seas and back from India, Arabia, and the east coast of Africa, into Europe. Trade's importance augured the civil-liability rule holding our boatman accountable for careless losses.

That trade brought the region remarkable riches. By the time of Nebuchadnezzar II who carried the Jews into exile from Jerusalem, three-and-a-half-foot square limestone slabs paved Babylon's streets, which led to palace walls of enameled or glazed brick as high as 30 feet, covered with animal figures. Belshazzar likely drank his demise from goblets pilloried from Jerusalem's Temple in one of Babylon's palace halls such as the Kasr, larger than a basketball court and with one wall 18 feet thick. Babylon was certainly the richest city of its day, with the most-advanced construction and engineering. Classical writers attributed

Babylon with fabled hanging gardens watered by a complex hydraulic screw. Our careless boatman plied the great brick-and-bitumen-lined canal that made a wide curve through the inner city wall into the city's heart, through sewage from the city's 200,000 population.

Hammurabi's law, order, and administrative ability promoted the economy. The splendor and enormity of the palaces and public works led our boatman to regard his society as the most advanced as possible. He certainly respected and may have feared its power and efficiency including the reach of its civil liability law for whatever cargo his carelessness lost. That cargo included grain, skins, lamp oil, dates, pottery, reeds, fish, milk, vegetables, wool, stone, bricks, leather, and people, indeed on occasion a naval force of king's soldiers. His river boat carried imported goods transferred from ship, including gold in rings, bags of alluvial gold deposits, silver in rings and ingots, copper, rock salt, iron, lead, and tin, wood, stone, and pearls. Horses, camels, ivory, elephant hides, and peacocks were other imports. Caravan was preferred transportation for larger animals. Slaves shipped and caravanned into the region from Africa. The variety and value of cargoes meant wide variance in losses. Cargoes, especially live cargoes, sometimes increased the hazards, when human and animal cargo distracted our careless boatman.

Language helps us understand the ancient civil-liability law governing our boatman because text recorded and communicated it, and allowed us to recover it. We credit Mesopotamians for inventing writing, first in Sumerian deciphered from clay cuneiform tablets excavated in large numbers throughout the region. The oldest tablets, first thought Semitic, were in a distinct language invading Sumerians brought to the region. Most tablets simply recorded quantities of dry goods, foodstuffs, and animals, with seal authenticating them as commercial record. Our careless boatman was quite familiar with recording and authenticating in accounting for cargoes. Tablets recording goods were Exhibit A in disputes over the value of cargoes his carelessness lost. Tradesmen also sealed with an impressed lump of clay doors, jars, and chests of goods for evidence of partial loss or damage.

In dealing with his accounts and civil liability, our boatman dealt with two languages. The earlier Sumerian added prefixes and suffixes to modify a single-syllable root for particular meanings. Hammurabi's Babylonian Semites recorded both Sumerian cuneiform and their own Akkadian language, sometimes on bilingual tablets. Akkadian differed from Sumerian in that it changed the internal structure of words as well as adding prefix and suffix for particular meanings. Akkadian gradually displaced Sumerian until Aramaic replaced Akkadian over a millennium later. Our boatman spoke Akkadian but recorded his transactions in both Sumerian and Akkadian. Hammurabi recorded the civil-liability law and other Code provisions on the great black stele and countless business tablets, in Sumerian cuneiform's pictorial lines and wedges. Over time, cuneiform lines and wedges began representing sounds, syllables, and letters more than the thing communicated. International trade influenced development of alphabetic characters, cuneiform gradually disappearing just before the time of Christ. Scholars could not decipher cuneiform until the mid-19th century, but our boatman knew and depended on it.

Writings were everywhere, including law writings. Babylon's temples held libraries to educate both scholars and children. Archaeologists even recovered archives of judicial decisions for reference in future cases. The temples also stored official government administrative records and decrees in clay or reed boxes. Businesses maintained their own day to day records on tablets sometimes in clay envelopes on shelves, depositing in large clay jars in the temple only their more-important documents. Our boatman's business documents contained many errors because of the linguistic gulf between street vernacular and written record, and the boatman's own modest writing skill. At home, his family stored tablets in cloth, reed mats, or household jars. While the writings had secular purpose, they bore sacred cast both because of writers' religious schooling and the moral Babylonian mindset Hammurabi's Code itself reflects deeply.

Our boatman read unrhymed but rhythmic Babylonian literature comprised of twin verses, like the Old Testament book Proverbs though of different origin. Literature included not only

34

poems, histories, conquest descriptions, hymns, prayers, and accounts of the gods but also exorcisms and incantations. Singing and storytelling preserved powerful tradition. Our boatman at times carelessly distracted himself in rhythmic sing-song tales to relieve his work's tedium and exertion but at other times sharpened his attention and restored his strength with hymns and prayers.

Shippers had the benefit of sound mathematics when our boatman's carelessness caused them loss. Babylonians used a numeric system based on the number ten that permitted something like decimals, although they did not yet recognize zero. Their mathematics included addition, subtraction, division, fractions, square and cube roots, geometry accurate to survey and calculate the areas of fields, and the Pythagorean Theorem one thousand years before Pythagoras. They knew pi's value quite accurately. Our boatman's year they divided into 360 days with 12 30-day months, adjusted from time to time by an additional month to conform the calendar to the 365-day solar year. Sound familiar? Our boatman had both sun- and water-clocks dividing the day into six two-hour parts with each two-hour period subdivided into 30 parts. We use the same Babylonian base 60 to tell time and measure circle degrees.

When injured, our boatman took medical treatment from priest physicians who supplemented prescriptions and applications made from plants, animals, and minerals, with incantations. They also performed lancing and external surgery. Overall, surprisingly little of language and learning distinguishes our ancient boatman's experience of civil liability from our own. Literature, writing, mathematics, calendar- and time-keeping, medicine, accounting, law, and lore were all integral to our boatman's daily expectations and experiences. We can now consider his civil-liability law with more confidence and context.

The word for *boatman* that Hammurabi's Code used, in Sumerian *ma-lah* and in Akkadian *malahu*, has no English equivalent. It describes not only a ship's navigator and ordinary seaman laborer but also a shipwright (builder of ships). The word that we translate as *boatman* obscures that the laws address the

35

rights and liabilities of four parties: (1) boat owner; (2) boat builder; (3) boat navigator; and (4) hirer of boats. This clarification helps us appreciate three key Babylonian-boatman laws including the careless-boatman provision, which we must interpret together to avoid confusion. Section 235 requires that the boat builder pitch the ship thoroughly to defeat rot and other defect, in the failure of which he must repair his defective work:

> If a boat-builder has built a boat for a man and his work is not firm, and in that same year that boat is disabled in use; then the boat-builder shall overhaul that boat, and strengthen it with his own material, and he shall return the strengthened boat to the boat-owner.

Here the law obviously deals with the work of the boat's builder in liability to the boat's owner. Section 236 then holds a navigator who leases a boat liable to its owner to replace it in the event of its negligent destruction:

> If a man has given his boat on hire to a boatman, and the boatman is careless, and the boat is sunk and lost; then the boatman shall replace the boat to the boat-owner.

Here the law deals with liability of navigator to owner. Section 237 then holds a boat's navigator liable to a shipper of goods (presumably a merchant) to replace both the boat and cargo in the event of their careless destruction:

> If a man has hired a boatman and ship, and with corn, wool, oil, dates, or whatever it be as freight, has freighted her, that boatman has been careless and grounded the ship, or has caused what is in her to be lost, the boatman shall render back the ship which he has grounded and whatever in her he has caused to be lost.

Easy it is to see why the navigator would replace the merchant's lost cargo: the merchant owned that cargo. Why though would the navigator replace the boat for the merchant who did not own it, especially after the previous §236 dealt with liability between navigator and owner? Section 237's provision requiring navigator to "render back the ship" to merchant assumes that merchant hired both navigator and boat, possibly for the one year for which Hammurabi's Code dictated rates of hire. The careless navigator owed not only for the merchant's lost cargo but for the merchant's lost opportunity to make use of the boat, in essence for lost profits. Our careless boatman's adversary merchant would have so construed §237.

The adjective *egu* stating the condition that the boatman must have been *careless* appears six times in the Code. Corresponding noun *megutu* meaning *neglect* or *negligence* appears once. Scholar translators agree that the Babylonian terms are the ancient equivalent of what today we call the lack of ordinary care, not taking the usual trouble, some form of laziness or inattention to recognized duty, or in a word, *negligence*. In addition to the careless-boatman provisions §§236 and 237, the Code uses the concept and condition of *negligence* in connection with: (1) a debtor failing to obtain a receipt for payment on account (§105); (2) a bailee failing to safeguard goods (§125); (3) a worker failing to return healthy a hired ox (§245); and (4) a herdsman failing to keep disease from his flock (§267). The Code uses four times a second phrase *ul egu ahi ul addi* to neglect or let one's arm drop: (1) Hammurabi in his epilogue claiming his due labor for his people's welfare; (2) the farmer who fails to cultivate land leased for that purpose (§44); (3) the landowner who fails to maintain a dyke causing its breach and flooding of adjacent lands (§53); and (4) the landowner who opens but forgets to close a sluice flooding his neighbor's lands (§55). These usages in so many obvious contexts leaves no doubt that they spoke of carelessness or negligence. Our boatman certainly understood the concept from the several common contexts in which the Code employed it.

The Code's prologue and epilogue repeatedly referring to *justice* reinforce that we must interpret the Code as requiring fitness for duty, proportion to obligation, fairness to others, and equity to one another. His Code stated that the gods entrusted Hammurabi to bring justice to his people, make justice appear in the land, destroy evil so that strong would not oppress weak, and promote truth and justice. His laws were just laws. The king of justice, he held a just scepter. Our boatman clearly understood Hammurabi's just intention. Law was indeed prominent in ancient Babylonia. Business documents show such broad range of legal terms widely in use that Babylonians, like us, were relatively litigious: heir, heiress, inheritance, and testament or will; to complain and have a claim against; lawsuit, to accept a lawsuit, to carry on a lawsuit, and to go before the judges; to compensate; just, justice, judgment, and to take, give, or pass judgment; court of justice, old court of justice, clerk at court of justice, and place giving oath; inconclusive evidence; to lose or forfeit; to redeem or buy back; to bind and be bound; to set free, give away, be free of an obligation, and be merciful; to support and give support; to honor and care; to appease; possession and deposit; sealed, stamped, sealed document, and scribe; marriage, dowry, and adoption; illegal and penalty; to borrow and loan; interest, to pay interest, and annual interest; to be at the command of; to entrust to another; and to divide, receive as a portion, and receive wrongly. Our boatman's counterparts certainly had sophisticated ability to communicate liability concepts.

Like us, Babylonians also gave considerable thought to how we came into being. Like us, they reached different conclusions. Short version of their creation legend had the earth covered with water until gods formed sanctuaries. The great god Bel-Marduk spread earth over reed mats he laid on the waters. He then formed man and with goddess Aruru formed the seed of mankind, followed by animals, Tigris and Euphrates Rivers, and vegetation. Alternative version began with watery nothingness out of which came gods in the form of men and devils occupying a close region. Warring of gods and devils followed. Universe mother Tiamat led the devils out of which the twelve zodiac signs arose. Gods anointed Marduk to battle with Tiamat's demonic legions. Marduk prevailed, wresting from devil captain the tablet recording every man's fate. Marduk then created man from the blood of Tiamat's god-husband Kingu, to have man make offerings to appease the gods' need for adulation. In return, the gods made Babylon shrine and abode for Marduk upon whom they bestowed their collective powers. Deities controlled Heaven. Sun and moon opened Heaven's doors. The god Ea occupied Earth while underworld gods inhabited subterranean region, governing spirits of the dead. Consider below how this cosmology affected our boatman's thinking.

First, though, appreciate divinity's Babylonian connotation. Babylonian gods took human and animal form, each god with its own characteristics and duties. Babylonians adopted most early Sumerian gods including the remote father-king god Anu, wind god Enlil, his son war god Ninurta, bird god Zu, fire and light god Makh, water god Enki, wise god Nabu, moon god Sin (fighter rather than incarnation of evil), sun god Shamash, storm god Mer, mother goddess Ishkhara, underworld gods Birtu and Manungal, and many others listed in a single record recovered from Nippur. Babylonians believed spirits in everything, some good, some bad, suggesting animism. Gifts appeased the spirits, especially local village god. Babylonians also referred to a singular God, even taking oaths before him, and at one point assigned powers of all gods to Marduk. *Babylon* derives from Sumerian *Ka Dingirra(ki)* Semitic Babylonians translated as *Babilu* or *Gate of God*. Our boatman thus recognized not only god pantheon but also lone great God.

That great Babylonian god Marduk, like the primary Assyrian god Ashur, was completely unlike the sublimely spiritual monotheistic Hebrew God. Babylonian cosmology was not monotheistic. The many Babylonian texts depiction no almighty, eternal, omniscient, just, unchanging, loving, and merciful father God. Even the great god Bel-Marduk to whom Nebuchadnezzar II credited his many achievements had a ceremonial equal in Nabu. The celebrated legend of part-god part-man Gilgamesh illustrates the complexity of Babylonian divinities, their interactions, and their influence upon men. Legend holds that Gilgamesh engaged in fantastic and heroic interplay with the gods even as he ruled his Babylonian people. One legend touches on our boatman's craft. Dreading death, Gilgamesh set out to discover from an immortal ancestor Uta-Napishtim death's nature and antidote. Goddess directed Gilgamesh to search out Uta-Napishtim's boatman for directions to his immortal ancestor. The boatman equipped Gilgamesh with a vessel, propelled with 120 punting poles so that each touched the Waters of Death only once, to reach Uta-Napishtim from whom Gilgamesh heard of the Flood that gained Uta-Napishtim immortality. The Waters of Death legend helped our careless boatman brave the rivers' natural hazards.

Our boatman may have accorded greater influence to the civil-liability law than religious influences. He did not shape his business behavior to please an ever-present, omniscient, omnibenevolent, creating, reasoning, judging, and loving God, whom he did not know. Omniscient, holy, intimate divinity beckons us to care even without influence from civil liability, although plenty of us continue in unduly hazardous action whenever we hope to escape human, if not divine, notice. Less than a natural law of love, our boatman followed an administrative dictate of civil liability for the absence of care. Our boatman nonetheless drew modifying influence from his divinities who expected his obedience to moral law. He made prayers and gave offerings to atone for offenses to that law, typically in private alone or on visits to the priest, not in public ceremony. Only, our boatman informed his morality not by eternal consequences to actions but by fear for supernatural response to his wrongs, and tempered his conduct accordingly.

Yet again, the civil-liability law had even greater influence on our boatman than due to the perceived absence of a God who both is and commands care. Our boatman had no conception of his own soul. Babylonian cosmology included no direct or general concept of human sin, repentance, and redemption. Babylonian conscience was more like that of the ancient Egyptian than Israelite. Commands and requirements of God and consequences of their violation differ from what our boatman drew from Bel-Marduk, Nabu, and subsidiary others. Bel-Marduk was, like the Egyptian Ra or Amen, lord of gods but not in any sense Lord like Hebrew God Jehovah and Son Jesus. Indeed, the Babylonian lord god descended in legend from monsters of foul form, far from the utterly pure, rational, loving, and pre-existent Hebrew God. Babylonians did not celebrate Bel-Marduk's mythical death, fall into hell, and rescue by god Enurta sent by god Anshar as Bel-Marduk's voluntary plan for human redemption. Babylonians took these legends as myth, not history, like the mythical death and resurrection of Egyptian god Osiris. They made no claim that their gods had intervened in human history after the manner of Abraham, Isaac, and Jacob, Pontius Pilate, tetrarch Herod, and Nazarene Jesus.

Our boatman also knew that legendary part-man, part-god Gilgamesh had not found immortality. Babylonian laborer had no intimation at any chance of life everlasting, even by strictest adherence to moral law no less than by interceding salvation. Babylonians anticipated spirit after-life in the underworld, not heaven. Our boatman believed gods to be gods, and boatmen to be boatmen, with no sense of divinity dwelling within boatmen. Babylonian gods concerned themselves with intricate, competitive, and even warring relationships among themselves. Men concerned Babylonian gods only incidentally, when gods might use human affairs profitably in divine events. Our boatman believed it possible and indeed highly desirable to escape god notice entirely, with no repentance and prayer other than to appease minor local gods.

Yet our boatman appealed to local gods in earnest. Each village had its own local god, increasingly venerated within growing temple of brick and imported stone as village swelled into town. Appreciate that out of one of these towns just south of the Euphrates River, Ur of the Chaldees, no less than the father of faith Abraham began his journey to the land the Hebrew One God promised him. Mesopotamians did regard commission of certain wrongs as offenses against the gods, deliverance from which required confession of sin. Babylonians expressed right and wrong differently from the generalized ethic drawn from the monotheistic God but not so differently. Our boatman had some concern for doing the right thing, as a matter of moral obligation. One distinction is that Hebrew practices lacked Babylonian ritual exorcism to rid one of sin. Ritual differs from relationship, but that distinction did not mean that our careless boatman was unconcerned with moral and supernatural consequences to his wrongs.

Indeed, the seated Babylonian sun god Shamash before whom Hammurabi stands on the famous fragments of the Code discovered at Susa in 1902, was to Babylonians judge of heaven and earth, a god of justice. Shamash named his two sons not depicted on the recovered monolith *Law* and *Justice*. The monolith depicts Shamash holding a stylus, the writing implement with which he recorded judgments. Babylonians saw the gods as lending order to natural chaos, kings as gods' terrestrial representatives, and law as a king's effort to carry out divine order. Thus our boatman may have been even more concerned with legal compliance than today's secular-minded citizens whom our modern civil liability laws subject.

Our boatman had other supernatural influences. Babylonian cosmology acknowledged spell weaving. One on whom a spell fell faced river dunking, sinking or swimming depending on spell guilt or innocence. Babylonians interwove magic with religion, unlike the holy Hebrew God's rejection of dark arts. *Interweaving* may be too generous a term. Babylonians had far greater concern for local spells and spirits than distant gods. Hammurabi regarded magic as an important science, closely connecting it with medicine in mixing sacrifices, amulets, and incantations with medicating waters, salves, and herbs. Babylonian prayers and incantations show greater concern for personal health, family relations, and general fortunes than for river navigation. Away from priests and family life, our careless boatman often felt that his river piloting needed not great deal more than his own attention. Yet given vagaries of flood and current, our boatman invested his work with circumspection for both divine and magical influences.

Government also influenced our boatman's thinking about civil liability and other laws. Hammurabi founded the Babylonian Empire. Under Hammurabi, the city of Babylon reached the zenith of its influence within and without Babylonia. Hammurabi ruled all of Babylon and Mesopotamia from the Tigris and Euphrates river deltas in modern-day Kuwait to the Mediterranean coast, before Hebrew nation emerged as political, legal, and social influence. Hammurabi's Babylon stretched from the river mouths northwestward to where fertile river deposits gave way to desert sand. The 100-foot-high, 20-foot-wide Median Wall from Takrit on Tigris to Hit on Euphrates marked Babylon's border.

Hammurabi did not rule as common despot, instead exhibiting great concern for those under his rule. He willingly considered the smallest administrative details as expressed in the justice and humanitarianism of his Code. His letters show the same concern. He imposed order by appointing trusted secular governors over his expanding districts, those governors communicating his law and order while reporting back with collected tax revenue. Hammurabi's order led to flourishing commerce and population increase until Babylonia became the world's central market. Our careless boatman plied his trade in vital international economy under world-leading government, in those respects like our own commerce. Babylonia's power declined rapidly after Hammurabi's death, though economic vitality disappeared only under Arab rule centuries later, as canal system disintegrated and region returned to depopulated desert.

Political history reflects how our ancient boatman regarded his government. Hammurabi was not the region's first ruler. Babylonian-predecessor Sumerian kings sometimes divided the land into northern and southern regions. Babylonians kept few records of those Sumerian kings, whose dynasties Elamite and Akkadian military defeats interrupted. Many records exist of Sumerian-ruler wars with Akkadians, to whom Sumerians gradually gave way by 2,450 B.C. Many records exist of the Akkadians who ruled in successions that eventually led to Hammurabi's rule because Akkadian kings deified themselves, a practice unusual for the region. Rulers and ruled typically regarded kings as men rather than divinities, unlike the Egyptian pharaohs who accepted the status of gods. Yet Babylonians did not entirely separate secular politics from sacred religion. High priest rather than secular governor would often rule a city and even when not would retain substantial control through the temple. Our careless boatman regarded the officials who enforced his civil-liability law as acting in both administrative and devout capacity.

Mesopotamian kings required the confidence of their subjects to suppress revolt. They did so through social justice reflecting concern for their subjects' welfare. The formula for king success was to heed justice, or subjects would rebel. Urukagina (ca. 2,800 B.C.) accordingly claimed that he "established the ordinances," Sargon (ca. 2751 B.C.) that he was "the king of justice" who "speaks justice," Ur-Engur (ca. 2450 B.C.) that he made "justice to prevail," and Lipit-Ishtar (ca. 2217 B.C.) that he "established justice." Our boatman appreciated that his willingness to accept the civil-liability law justified it. Law did not come entirely from gods or kings but in part from the degree to which its subjects recognized its fitness to their everyday relations. Conquerors did not always strip vanquished cities. Akkadian ruler Dungi (ca. 2,150 B.C.), for example, established standard weights and measures in conquered cities to impress inhabitants with his equity and foresight. Semite rulers equally did so including those who began a Babylonian dynasty in 2,057 B.C. lasting for about 300 years. Hammurabi was the sixth king of this 11-king Semitic dynasty. We cannot know the extent to which his civil-liability law aided in the social justice typical of these dynastic rulers, though its inclusion in his Code and other codes indicates its importance. Our boatman accepted the negligence provision under which he worked as one socially just law in a social-justice system ensuring the orderly trade on which he depended, perhaps much like commercial haulers recognize motor-vehicle negligence law today.

Rulers exercised judicial power in addition to political and administrative power. Records of judgments over debts, sales, slaves, compensation for damage, marriages, revenues, failure to plant lands, divorce, and other disputes begin with early 24th-century-B.C. Akkadian rulers. One collection of consecutive tablets recovered from Ur domestic quarters record disputes arising from the purchase of a slave, from theft, out of a partnership, from a deposit, out of a marriage, from the purchase of a calf, from the purchase of various children of both sexes, and from loans and contracts. No record exists of boat or cargo loss lawsuits. The most interesting of the Ur legal records for our purposes is the record one litigant kept for damages received (both gold and barley) in a lawsuit with a brewer. Yet these plentiful and varied legal records strongly suggest that our boatman respected the judicial means to administer and enforce the civil-liability provision to which he was subject.

Legal procedure was sophisticated for what one would expect of ancient society. Trial was before local council comprised of village elders and mayor or by judges appointed from those ranks.

Elders and judges made frequent judicial decisions, often enough that they possessed adequate skill and experience even when without access to judicial archives. Trial was at the city gate or temple courtyard rather than in any building designated as court. Parties introduced documentary exhibits, gave their own account, and called other witnesses who swore to the gods to tell the truth but faced no cross-examination. Witnesses also testified by deposition. Some records show citizens sitting with council judges similar to an early jury and of matters brought before the whole town. Scribes transcribed records of civil cases for damages. Parties could delay for months to compel witness attendance by party effort or letter from judge to local authority. Witnesses had the Code's protection. Death penalty threatened anyone coercing a witness, although little evidence exists to show capital sentence carried out. Judges who accepted bribes faced fine and expulsion. Councils announced decisions publicly unless referring a matter to higher regional or palace authority. Appeals could go all the way to the king who had ultimate responsibility for administration of justice, though kings often referred disputes back to local authorities. Hammurabi himself presided over and supervised cases. Soldiers enforced judgments. Heralds who announced decisions also presided over sales of forfeited property. Merchants consigning our boatman's cargo occasionally threatened him with these procedures.

Not so sophisticated were the trials by river ordeal for certain cases not resolved by judicial means. Hammurabi's Code authorized trial by ordeal. It involved a ritual vigil followed by a recitation of the facts requiring the ordeal, the party's plunge into the river, search for the body if the party did not emerge, and display of the bloodied corpse providing suitable deterrent to wrongdoers. When civil disputants on both sides survived the watery trial, relative merits of their opposing claims depended on the distance they swam before emerging. Humanely, litigants could abandon claims in the course of ordeal to avoid demise of additional parties. Trial by ordeal gave far greater incentive to resolve claims than various modern means of procedural leverage such as offer-of-judgment sanctions. Ordeal lent authority to law,

45

especially in our boatman's eyes as he witnessed ordeals and aided in search for grisly verdict.

Babylonia's justice system had remarkable political stability. Hammurabi was not the last of the powerful and just rulers. Three Babylonian dynasties of considerable influence succeeded the 11-king dynasty of which Hammurabi's reign was the jewel. The Babylonian dynasties that followed held so little influence that Assyrians to the north displaced them using brutal methods of quelling rebellion that cowed the once-mighty Babylonians. Assyrian dominance eventually waned until 625 B.C. when Babylonians once again set their own king on the throne. Shortly after, Babylonian king Nebuchadnezzar II (namesake to the great Babylonian king Nebuchadnezzar of 400 years earlier in the last of the powerful Babylonian dynasties) destroyed the Jewish Temple in Jerusalem, carrying the Jews into exile after their rebellion, refusal to pay tribute, and rejection of Babylonian political influence. Not long after in 538 B.C., Persian king Cyrus dealt Babylonia its last great defeat, although it would be more than a thousand years hence in 635 A.D. that Arabs gained the broken land's full control, establishing Baghdad as their capital. Our boatman within his own short life span regarded Babylonian dynasty permanent fixture.

Local politics held more interest and importance for our careless boatman than these regional concerns. Rivers and geography made for local conflict. Huge deserts east and west imbalanced resources. Desert marauders carried off grain, livestock, and women from the rich river towns whenever dynastic rulers and governors relaxed security. Especially in early times, city chiefs fought with neighboring chiefs for control along the rivers. Our boatman tried to avoid but occasionally fell into local conflicts. Cities remained flourishing commercial centers. Our boatman gained direct benefit from Hammurabi's peace and order, enough to accept its civil-liability regulation.

Now consider directly Babylonian laws of which our careless boatman's civil-liability provision was part. Common law comprised of the habits of judges in individual cases was well established and developed in the region by around 3,000 B.C.

46

Babylonian law included religious, moral, and civic law. Religious law required worship and service to divinities. Moral law demanded that our boatman and others speak truly, honor parents, and not murder, commit adultery, rob, or deceive. Civic law specified and applied moral law, prohibiting cheating with false weights and measures, trespass, moving boundary marks, destroying another's crops, stopping up watercourses, and other acts causing injury or loss to others. Royal verdicts and decrees balanced equities, modifying or amplifying liabilities as circumstances compelled. Our careless boatman's civil liability provision lay in this morals-based civic law.

The civil liability and other social laws were in no sense anomalous. Hammurabi's Sumerian predecessor by 500 years Urukagina memorialized his extensive social reforms in a law code that included abating sacred abuses, bribery, and oppression of peasants by priestly and official classes. Fragments of an ancient Sumerian family code suggest again that civil provisions compelling consideration of other interests were common. As the prior chapter shows, civil liability was part of the earlier Laws of Eshnunna from the same region. Three-fourths of the other Laws of Eshnunna also appeared with only slight difference in Hammurabi's Code. Babylonian scholars knew the earlier Sumerian codes. Ur-Nammu of the last of the powerful Sumerian dynasties was a talented administrator who in addition to promulgating the earliest known law code also maintained a ship registry to protect them from southern marauders.

Our careless boatman certainly did not escape official notice, protection, and regulation centuries later during Hammurabi's even more-efficient administration. Ur-Nammu's laws contain a prologue much like Hammurabi's in which Ur-Nammu boasts of putting an end to exploitation of the poor, widowed, and orphaned, and of restoring justice. Mesopotamians appreciated justice in its particular applications. On Hammurabi's conquest, he commanded compilation of Sumerian and Akkadian laws then extant into the single code that we know as the Code of Hammurabi. Hammurabi placed the original of his code in the Marduk's Temple. Archaeologists discovered a copy from another temple at Susa in what is now Iran millennia later in 1902.

Three years earlier Babylonian scholar Delitzsch predicted the Code's discovery from remnants 1,000 years more recent. Delitzsch correctly guessed that Hammurabi had ordered the Code's compilation. Shortly later, French excavations at Susa unearthed three large fragments of inscribed stone that when assembled formed a seven-foot-tall, six-foot-in-circumference black diorite pillar.

On the pillar Hammurabi had inscribed archaic Babylonian hieroglyphics in their characteristic wedge-shaped forms. The top of the pillar bears a relief of Hammurabi standing before the seated Babylonian sun god of justice Shamash. The pillar's Elamite plunderer (probably Shutruk-Nakhunte, ca. 1100 B.C.) scratched out five columns of the inscription, intending to inscribe his own memorial after bringing the pillar from Babylonia to Susa. The pillar originated in a temple at Larsam or Sippara, as a copy of the original Code that Hammurabi erected at Babylon in the great Temple. Scholars date the copy, now in the Louvre in Paris, to just before 1750 B.C.

The Code begins with Hammurabi's tribute to the gods Anu, Bel, Ea, and Ea's son Marduk to whom the gods granted their powers. The tribute acknowledges that the gods gave Hammurabi reign "to make justice to prevail in the land, to overthrow wickedness and evil, to relieve the weak from the oppression of the strong," and "to illumine the land, and to promote the well-being of men." The Code was remarkably modern in its expressed purpose, which people today would accept but for unfamiliar divine references. We might think of our careless boatman as a good ordinary citizen for having the same spirit as that which Hammurabi's dedication expressed. The prologue then listed the cities and temples Hammurabi had rebuilt, only then embarking on its enumerated 280 provisions. Though prologue made frequent references to the divine, the laws themselves show such absence of divine reference as to be wholly secular in nature, unlike the Hebrews' laws having contrastingly clear sacred purpose.

Hammurabi's Code organized its body of laws. The first 5 sections had to do with administration of justice, next 20 with offenses against property, next 50 with land use, next 40 with trade, next 68 with family life, next 20 with assault, next 16 with professional services, next 16 with oxen, next 11 with agriculture and herdsmen, next 10 with rates of hire, and last 5 with slaves. Administrators and our boatman knew the civil-liability law as only one in a series of provisions establishing social order and justice. Hammurabi's Code did not take the form of law prohibitions but was instead a collection of if-then statements. This feature, together with the absence from that period of any word for *law*, suggests that Babylonians conceived not of general law principles but instead individual judgments. The prologue cast Hammurabi as a social reformer so that we should interpret the judgments as reforms to the common law.

On the other hand, from its introduction, content, and organization, the Code was not a series of actual judgments (of which we have many other records) but instead to collect and communicate representative judgments officials should make in the given cases. For instance, several consecutive striking-a-pregnant-woman judgments show the writer extending a basic injunction to teach principle more than single case rule. As Hammurabi himself stated in conclusion, "if that [judge] has the sanction (of the gods) and so is able to give his land justice, let him pay heed to the words which I have written on my stele, and let that stele show him the accustomed way, the way to follow...." Officials who administered the careless-boatman law saw their action as pursuit of fitting god-sanctioned judgment. The Code is not our only source for understanding Babylonian law, though. Contract documents for transport of goods by water also show its working. Contracts were oral, written, and also symbolized by act such as striking the forehead in guarantee of transaction. The parties described agreements, acts, and transactions in signed, witnessed, and sealed documents.

The Code had an almost unimaginably lasting impact. Two thousand years after its origin, Babylonians still used it to study law, while Assyrians continued its use into the 7th century B.C. The order Hammurabi imposed enabled women to travel safely from Babylon to the Mediterranean, protecting both rich and poor in person and property through safe transit certainly not possible today over the same route and instead more like U.S. travel. Oddly, though we have many ancient copies of Hammurabi's Code, individual decisions make but a single reference to the Code itself, likely more evidence that the Code guided decisions rather than mandated actions as modern statutory code would. Babylonians did not know the concept of a statutory code but instead took guidance from decisions, as the Code itself stated and its persistent reproduction through the ages reflected. The Code certainly impacted local councils and judges administering civil justice.

Our concern though is that of the civil-liability law on our careless boatman. How did our boatman regard compliance with the law? Hammurabi had an advantage over rulers today. Mesopotamians valued obedience as prime virtue. While Hammurabi professed concern to protect the weak from oppression, the norm was not individual rights but submission to authority. Complying with law, obeying authority, and paying taxes remain prime virtues today in religious writings, although less so in secular society pursuing self-directed liberty. Our boatman may have been more obedient. Ancients were on the other hand human and thus subject to ordinary lapses, greed, selfishness, and other vices that could readily cause loss or harm. Harm and loss were then and today remain likely, but the boatman's willingness to comply with civil-liability law may have been greater. We may care less for obedience, more for ourselves, and less for others than did ancient Babylonian boatman.

Our boatman knew that the civil-liability law could affect his own interests and that he ought to direct his efforts accordingly. An example available to us has not to do directly with boatmen but with a land dispute during the reign of Hammurabi's successor. A priestess claimed land by inheritance from an aunt who had allegedly bought the land 52 years earlier from the opposing claimant's father. The opposing claimant advocated that his father had sold only part of the land. With no surviving witnesses to the sale, city registrar and judges decided the dispute by examining the original sale tablet. In the day's customary method, impression of the seller's and buyer's seals over the original inscription protected the tablet from alteration. They had

50

also sealed the tablet within a clay envelope separately impressed with the terms of sale and then sealed over. Ancient envelopes, opened after excavation, have shown suspicious differences between outside and inside inscriptions. On opening this envelope, judges found the plot described as priestess claimed. Priestess received judgment in her favor with opposing claimant forbidden to reopen the dispute. Civil dispute into which our careless boatman fell would, if not voluntarily resolved, resolve by similar judicial proceeding and judgment.

We thus glimpse the life of a careless boatman. Consciousness seems a strange thing. Inferences we draw of the civil-liability law's meaning to boatmen are probably hazardous. Is judging another's heart from economy, family structure, language, and other social forms ever really possible? Yet what the above study suggests by the surprisingly similar life the boatman had to our own, at least in its social if not technological aspects, is that the influence and function of his civil-liability law might well have been much like our own law. The boatman's care and carelessness may have meant to the boatman much the same as they mean to us today. We discover from a study of this kind that ages and cultures must share certain laws, and especially such a basic law of civility, because those laws define humanity. As much as Babylonians had distinct geography, economy, technology, cosmology, language, and culture, their civil-liability law may nonetheless have operated much like our own as an ageless constant. Care may not be mere social or legal convention. The standard to which we of all ages appeal instead transcends us.

Chapter 3

A Moral Tradition

As we shall see in greater detail later, conventional wisdom today and for the past 100 years has been that law generally and tort law in particular originated in mythology or theology. Only gradually (the story goes) did tort law become secular as humanity shed its superstitions. The above evidence of ancient tort law suggests the contrary that tort law existed from the earliest recovered records in secular commercial states. Tort law did not have a theistic or superstitious origin but was present from our beginning because of ordinary necessity. Yet now we shall see that theology entered later with impact. Our relationship to the eternal divine raised the stakes for law generally as for tort law in particular. Though schools and commentators ignore tort law's biblical heritage, when the American Bar Association recently convened a special committee to study the tort system, its 1,000-page report began by recognizing that the Old Testament fills with tort rules. Consider what those rules provided.

American law's abiding debt to its Judeo-Christian heritage makes imperative that we consider the Old Testament's Book of the Covenant, or Covenant Code. The Covenant Code lies within Exodus, the second book of the Jewish Torah or Pentateuch and the Old Testament within the Christian Bible. Scholars attribute the Torah to Moses, meaning that it follows by several centuries the Laws of Eshnunna and Code of Hammurabi but is still more than three millennia old. Moses wrote the Covenant Code in the Semitic language of Hebrew. Hebrew relates to Semitic Akkadian in which the Laws of Eshnunna and Code of Hammurabi appear.

Indeed, study shows similarity between the earlier laws and the Covenant Code. Compare the goring-ox rule of Hammurabi's Code, "If a man's ox (was) a gorer and the ward have had made known to him that (it was) a gorer, but he did not screen its horns, (or) did not tie up his ox and that ox gored a son of a man and caused him to die, he shall give ½ a mina of silver," with the Covenant Code provision, "But if the ox was previously reputed to have had the propensity to gore, and its owner had not kept it under control, he shall make good ox for ox, but will keep the dead one for himself." Both laws concern failure to guard against known risk, with compensation for resulting damage.

Oddly, though, scholars cannot trace the earlier laws to the later. A gap of several hundred years exists between them without any linking text. The laws also appear within completely different systems, the earlier in cuneiform, the latter in the alphabetic style derived from Egyptian hieroglyphics. Moses recorded the Covenant Code in Palestine at the edge of Mesopotamian influence where Egyptian and Mesopotamian cultures met and overlapped. Despite the laws' similarity, they also have important differences, as we shall see after we first consider a brief survey of the Covenant Code's tort provisions.

The Covenant Code includes at least eight negligence or tort-like rules involving: 1) spreading fire; 2) straying livestock; 3) uncovered pit; 4) bull goring bull; 5) bull goring human; 6) not maintaining railing around roof to prevent fall; 7) injury by swinging axe; and finally, 8) injury during quarrel. For instance, the spreading-fire provision at Exodus 22:6 states, "If a fire breaks out and spreads into thorn bushes so that it burns shocks of grain or standing grain or the whole field, the one who started the first must make restitution." The rule does not mention the fire-starter's carelessness. It may imply carelessness or could be a strict-liability provision. The rule is not clear, as our tort rules today are not always clear. Strict products liability under the American Law Institute's Restatement (Second) of Torts §402A provides liability for products that injure without respect to fault but also requires that claimants prove the product in defective condition unreasonably dangerous, in essence a negligence requirement.

The Covenant Code's straying-livestock provision comes closer to a sure negligence provision, at Exodus 22:5 stating, "If a man grazes his livestock in a field or vineyard and lets them stray and they graze in another man's field, he must make restitution from the best of his own field or vineyard." This rule more clearly infers a negligence requirement that the herder has carelessly allowed livestock to stray. Although the rule makes no direct mention of carelessness, one does not *let* something happen without capability of stopping it. The term *straying* also implies careless departure from controlled herd, again suggesting negligence. The rule is also clear that the straying animal's owner pays for harm the animal wrought, plainly a civil-liability rule.

The Covenant Code's uncovered-pit rule at Exodus 21:33-34 is even clearer in deterring carelessness, stating, "If a man uncovers a pit or digs one and fails to cover it and an ox or a donkey falls into it, the owner of the pit must pay for the loss; he must pay its owner, and the dead animal will be his." The rule gives two negligence examples, first as careless action to uncover covered pit and second as careless omission to fail to cover new-dug pit. Both act and omission neatly characterize the rule as one against carelessness. The rule also specifically prescribes compensation commensurate with the dead animal's value, thus indisputably making it a civil-liability rule.

Two more Covenant Code provisions imply fault as condition for liability and compensation as remedy. The Code's parapet-round-roof rule at Deuteronomy 22:8 states, "When you build a new house, make a parapet around your roof so that you may not bring the guilt of bloodshed on your house if someone falls from the roof." Not to guard one's roof against falls presumes carelessness in a hot region where spending a cool evening on the roof would have been usual. The rule leaves unstated the civil penalty for violation, presumably compensation like the other rules. The injured-worker provision at Exodus 21:18-19 states, "If men quarrel and one hits the other with a stone or with his fist and he does not die but is confined to bed, the one who struck the blow will not be held responsible if the other gets up and walks around outside with his staff; however, he must pay the injured man for the loss of his time and see that he is completely healed."

Here, the rule compels compensation, though basing liability not on carelessness but intent, associating quarrel with ill will.

The Covenant Code thus clearly includes tort rules like those we know today, considering both conditions for liability and compensation as remedy. Wrongdoer pays wronged to compensate for loss whether loss involves personal property, real property, or other economic interest. The liability condition is typically negligent act or omission, or in one rule harmful intent. Comparing the earlier ox-goring rules, we see in the Covenant Code similar conditions for notice ("if the ox was previously reputed to have had the propensity to gore"), knowledge ("its owner having been so warned"), carelessness ("yet he did not keep it under control"), and monetary compensation ("he must pay thirty shekels of silver"). The Covenant Code's tort rules seem plain and purposeful enough if also somewhat simple or rough, as some scholars would today regard them.

Yet biblical law is not quite so simple. We should not construe the Torah within which we find these tort rules or the larger Old Testament as reflecting the ancient Israelites' mundane commercial concerns. Indeed, anything but. Hammurabi intended his Code to govern commerce and economic life. By contrast, the Torah and larger Old Testament are instead sacred works. They caution that their purpose includes setting the Israelites utterly apart from ordinary life. Unlike Hammurabi's Code, the Old Testament is not a commercial code or case precedent, not primarily to state ordinary commercial norms in any comprehensive sense. It is rather a *testament*. One could even say that Covenant Code regulations are merely incidental to its sacred purpose. We must therefore take much greater care extrapolating broad legal norms from the Old Testament than from the earlier Code of Hammurabi.

For that reason, we should not be so quick to imply negligence as a condition to recovery in the Covenant Code's tort rules. Contemporary tort law would in the absence of negligence mostly let loss fall where it may. By contrast, we could read the Covenant Code's fire, stray, pit, roof, ox, and axe rules by their strict terms to permit liability without such negligence. The ancient Hebrews may have been able under their sacred Code to insist that loss distribution occur even without negligence. After all, it could be unfair to make the dead ox's owner carry all of the loss, when the goring ox's owner had shared in the enterprise that created risk and concomitant loss. Restoration of community equilibrium, deterring of self-help, preservation of peace, and loss-spreading policies all justify strict liability. Disorder introduced by these events could affront the Hebrews' uniquely holy God who might require participants to set right those wrongs. Secular rules may not satisfy sacred ends. Divine relationship requires something more from tort law.

Consecration affected tort law more than in just widening civil liability's scope. It also affected tort remedies. Formerly, rich could buy the life or limb of poor by compensating at regulated amounts torts committed against them. Yet the Covenant Code's goring-ox rules upped the ante. The Covenant Code provides at Exodus 21:28 that for an ox that gores the first time, the ox must be stoned to death, which would not be the usual manner of killing an ox, and its remains discarded, which would not be the usual manner of treating available meat: "If an ox gores a man or woman to death, the ox shall be stoned to death, its flesh may not be eaten, but the owner of the ox is innocent." For the most egregious case when the ox owner's negligent failure to control the ox already known to gore resulted in a person's death, the Covenant Code at Exodus 21:29 requires not only stoning of the ox but further that ox owner should die unless paying a ransom:

> But if the ox was previously reputed to have had the propensity to gore, its owner having been so warned, yet he did not keep it under control, so that it then killed a man or a woman, the ox shall be stoned to death, and its owner shall be put to death as well. Should a ransom be imposed upon him, however, he shall pay as the redemption for his life as much as is assessed upon him. Whether it shall have gored a minor [a son or a daughter] this same rule shall apply to him.

Why add penalties rather than apply usual rules of negligence, compensation, satisfaction, and release? Consider again the Covenant Code's sacred context. Stoning was ritual extirpation of public offense, a *sacred* rather than civil offense. Money may cure civil wrongs between mortal private parties, but money does not satisfy holy God whose supreme mortal-creating, law-giving authority sacred offense transgresses. Sacred offenses requiring greater payment than mere money include worship of foreign gods (Deuteronomy 13:7ff) or astral bodies (Deuteronomy 17:2-7), disobedient son (Deuteronomy 21:18-21), promiscuous bride (Deuteronomy 22:20f), fornicating couple betrothed to others (Deuteronomy 22:23f), sedition against king (1 Kings 21), and violation of Sabbath (Exodus 32:12-18). Civil law does not even recognize these torts.

Yet in each such case, the Old Testament ordained stoning, which is a sacred rather than civil edict. Stoning preserved the hierarchy of God over man and in the goring-ox case man over animal, preserving the community's moral standing without which it had no claim to exist. Stoning set apart the Hebrews as God's chosen people. Sacred stoning had no place in secular Laws of Eshnunna and Code of Hammurabi. Indeed stoning's only place in the Covenant Code's goring-ox rules was to correct offense to God, not to compensate dead-ox owner. One corrects awful offense against God only by awful stoning remedy. The Covenant Code preserves pecuniary payment for negligent wrongs like ox goring ox the harm from which would not offend sacred order. What the untrained eye would see as innocuous or coarse difference between ancient secular and sacred texts instead demonstrates different underlying rationales. Tort law's bottom line remains that one whose negligence causes harm should pay. Yet other, higher reasons now compelled a different, higher payment.

Other Covenant Code provisions have equally subtle liability rules. Exodus 21:35-36 contrasts a Solomon-like, strict-liability, divide-the-ox rule when the owner did not know the ox to gore with a pay-for-the-whole-ox, negligence-liability rule where the owner knew the ox to gore:

> If an ox belonging to one man gores to death the ox of his fellow, they shall sell the live ox and divide the proceeds, and they shall divide the dead one as well. But if the ox was previously reputed to have had the propensity to gore, and its owner had not

kept it under control, he shall make good ox for ox, but will keep the dead one for himself.

These distinctions in remedy between strict liability and negligence liability seem sensible, indeed more sensitive than our own tort rules, which tend to provide no compensation whatsoever in the absence of negligence, an all-or-nothing proposition not very satisfactory to losers. Appropriately, the Covenant Code reserves strict liability to property damage including only beasts or produce. Digging a pit into which another's animal falls, killing another's ox, cattle taking pasture in another's field, and fire spreading to another's lands each warrant more-expansive strict liability. So should rules be in an agrarian society with replaceable beasts and produce. Loss circumstances could be difficult to prove. Loss in any circumstance might as well warrant strict liability, which is enterprise liability, just as law strict products liability provides today for our plenteous products.

The Covenant Code's rules for indirect damage involving pit, ox, cattle, and fire divide into two groups, (1) pit and ox as to which liability depends on ownership, and (2) cattle and fire as to which liability depends on acts. Ownership of pit and goring ox are conditions for partial restitution simply because of the enterprise associated with ownership. Profitable enterprises bearing risks should pay associated costs. Ownership of *uncovered* pit and *known-dangerous* ox, negligence aggravating the wrong, require greater compensation in full restitution. The Covenant Code's apt subtleties make modern tort rules on cattle and fire seem rudimentary or even arbitrary.

Just because the Covenant Code does not include more-general liability rules for other property damage and personal injury does not mean that the rules did not exist. The Covenant Code's silence may suggest only that other rules were so obvious and necessary as to require no textual treatment, or that the associated wrongs did not transgress the sacred requiring inclusion in an indisputably sacred rather than secular text. Indeed by Rabbinic times, the Talmud had filled these seeming gaps in the text. The Talmud as Jewish lore arose in the centuries after Christ until complete in the sixth century. The Talmud treats the Torah's spreading fire, straying livestock, uncovered pit, and goring bull as archetypes, from which the Talmud derives categories of negligence. The Talmud interprets these archetypes to provide that a person is liable only for damage due to negligence, not for accidental damage.

Specifically, the Talmud at BK 21b, 52a/b, and 99b defines negligence to mean conduct that the wrongdoer should foresee will likely cause harm. The Talmud articulates an objective standard of care around what ordinarily intelligent and capable persons normally foresee. If the harm is one not normally foreseen, then no negligence exists. If the one claiming harm should have foreseen and avoided it, then again no negligence liability exists. The Talmud illustrates the absence of negligence: animal falls into a pit the cover for which had decayed, BK 52a; wall or tree falls onto highway without warning, BK 6b; and fire spreads further than foreseeable, BK 61b. Under these three provisions, negligence liability arises only after dangerous condition exists long enough for reasonable owner to discover. The Talmud provides for other modern-seeming tort rules for indirect damage, unusual damage, liability defenses, and joint wrongdoers. Because Jewish scholars assembling the Talmud drew such rules from the Torah, then so should we.

Where one might misinterpret the Torah to authorize disproportional remedy, the Talmud supplements the text to restore proportion. For example, Mishnah Baba Qamma 3.9 provides that "[i]f an ox worth 100 zuz gored an ox worth 200 zuz, and the carcass [the usual remedy] was worth nothing, the injured [party] takes the other ox." The Talmud repeatedly concludes not only that the Torah included general tort rules but further that the Torah's rules supplied sensitive justice even in seeming anomaly. For another example, while the Covenant Code commands death for the negligent owner of a man-killing ox, Talmud Tractates Baba Qamma 40b and 40c construe the command as moral condemnation while transforming alternative ransom into pecuniary obligation. The Talmud converts inflexible religious condemnation into flexible private accommodation, and not incidentally, the same private accommodation through civil

60

liability that we make today. The wronged holds the wrongdoer ransom subject to the judiciary's modifying influence.

When scrutinizing old tort laws, we must know enough of the society's social, cosmological, and theological views, its culture, and how its institutions reflect individual commitments and conscience. Above chapters show how in transposing Mesopotamian rules into their own theological framework, Israelites transformed the rules into different meanings and applications. Unlike distant competing Mesopotamian deities, the immanent and rational Israelite God would bless those whose devotion led to their following his laws. Thus Israelites read similar laws differently. Whether as Mesopotamians and Israelites then or moderns now, we project ourselves out on law, meaning that we must know to whom the law applies to understand how it actually operates.

We must also take care when we refer to *Laws* of Eshnunna and the *Code* of Hammurabi that we do not mistakenly impose modern-code constructs on ancient text without asking whether those constructs properly reflect use of ancient text. The above chapter showed that Mesopotamian codes stated hypothetical situations concluding with normative or corrective act. We should not assume that situations the ancient codes described commonly occurred or that the ancients uniformly or ever enforced the rules. The situations they addressed may have been apocryphal, and the norms they reflected or imposed might have been aspirational or admonitory in ways different from modern laws. The above chapter showed that the Covenant Code's law-like provisions dictated conduct of man toward God and man toward man not in secular fashion but religious context.

Consider how some might misread an Old Testament text on animal trials. The above chapter showed that Exodus 21:29's goring-ox rule required stoning ox, from which some might draw that primitive mind attributed guilty ox with animistic will. Yet the rule the rule implied no such ridiculous sense that ox should have known better and thus bore culpable guilt. The Israelites did not put animals on trial, and if they had, they would not have done so because of animistic beliefs. Modern procedural mindset might infer stoning ox meant ox guilt, when Israelite would instead see ritual act restoring sacred order. The Old Testament was theological not procedural work. Hammurabi's Code had no rule for putting animals on trial. That the Code predated the Old Testament by several hundred years and that Old Testament writers knew of the Code should put to rest the modern view that the primitive mind had not yet discerned a difference between human sentience and animal innocence. No more validity lies in that misjudgment of ancient laws than if one assumed that obviously comic Shakespeare scenes were literal, making tragedy of farce.

Law writings also held only limited place in ancient society. Ancient recorders of law codes knew that others would not widely read and follow them and that codes would have little immediate effect. The incomplete codes were not legislative edicts. Only later when Torah became identified with Greek concept of law *nomos* did it begin to function more like modern law. Oral law regulated ancient social life. Codifiers had different aims, not to create comprehensive law encyclopedia but to record examples that would celebrate ruler justice, as testament rather than code. Not until the later Greeks do we find written law as comprehensive binding rule enforced by regime, although ancient records did function for review and ordering. We better treat ancient texts not as comprehensive code but judgment list, which happens to be their peculiar form. We should make the best, not the worst, of ancient tort-law texts.

Treat ancient texts sensitively as to language employed not to impose historical and philosophical bias. Daube conjectures that if scholars saw how Old Testament texts use causative verbs, which ancient Hebrew forms from adjectives and nouns more readily than modern English, they would not have overlooked how sensitively ancient rules treated causation. Example is Exodus 21:30's goring-ox rule that negligent owner of known gorer that has killed may ransom his life by pecuniary payment. The offense against God required extirpation of offenders, both ox as out-of-order chattel and negligent owner. Exodus 21:30 used Hebrew word *kofer* for ransom or commutation rather than payment, followed by *pidyon* for redemption rather than compensation, indicating to philologist Finkelstein that the measures addressed religious redemption rather than secular compensation. That victim's age had nothing to do with ransom price ("Whether it shall have gored a minor this same rule shall apply to him," Exodus 21:30) confirms focus on redemption rather than compensation. Ransom only incidentally also served secular negligence deterrence and victim compensation. Recognize subtle and profound implications of word choice.

Consider the effect on ancient laws of transition from oral to literary culture. Ancient oral narratives, which early codes typify, preserve typical images and stories of the day. Those narratives work only in their cultural context, which is the only context in which their speakers would expect them to apply. By contrast, we more easily interpret generally, out of any peculiar context, texts published in widely literate society, where writers would know that they must fix meaning within the transferable medium for readers whose context writers would not readily know. The thief rule of Exodus 22:2-3 illustrates this contrast between oral narrative and literary text. Exodus 22:2-3 provides, "If the thief is found breaking in, and is struck so that he dies, there shall be no bloodguilt for him. But if the sun has risen upon him, there shall be bloodguilt for him." The first verse permits deadly force in defense of homestead whenever thief broke in, whereas second verse permits force only before sunrise, contradiction the literal text does not reconcile. Job 24:14, 16, which ancient hearer would have known, provides explanatory context that the thief "rises in the dark, that he may kill the poor and needy; and in the night he is as a thief." To hearer of oral tradition, thief rose and wrought mischief in dark. Job's thief definition readily explains Exodus's omission when the two books were integral parts of single oral tradition. To treat them as independent is to treat them as modern text when they were instead unitary oral tradition. Interpret ancient oral traditions in their context.

Do not read modern processes and institutions into ancient law. To treat ancient laws fairly, recognize their institutional context. Ancient judges accommodated justice over literal application of text, as urged in Deuteronomy 16:18, Deuteronomy 17, 2 Chronicles 17, 19, 19:6, Proverbs 16:10, and 1 Samuel 7:15-8:3, admonishing judges to deliver righteous judgment, avoid partiality, pursue justice, and not follow rules or even case precedents. Ancient laws also preferred private settlement over judicial decision on public rules. Parties tended to resolve differences in private communication around shared values, of necessity due to communication and travel limitations. Ancients avoided courts in favor of private adjudication under shared laws they saw as self-executing. In that context so unlike our own, one readily sees benefit of objective tests like Exodus 22:2-3's for night-time defense of homestead.

Another example is Exodus 21:18-19's self-executing rule that once battery victim rises from bed after recovering from blow, causation ends as to any subsequent death, liability remaining only for loss of wage until the victim rose. As clear as it is, the rule would seldom require fact adjudication. Today medical technology enables us to determine medical causation far more reliably, and so we have broader fact-based medical-causation rules. Today we adjudicate in courts applying public written rules, that modern process preserving autonomy and promoting accountability but sacrificing sense of privately-held, shared values. Each system fit the day's technology, institutions, and culture.

Any study of Covenant Code tort rules though must consider its most prominent feature. Everyone associates the Code's eye-for-eye, tooth-for-tooth remedy with Old Testament justice. Indeed this remedy that scholars label *talion* is obstacle to modern mind accepting Old Testament subtlety, sensitivity, and richness. Talion's eye-for-eye justice invokes primitive religion, redeemed only by conjecture that talion limited (rather than authorized) more-awful vengeance of savage ancient mind.

Discovery of sensitive Sumerian and Akkadian pre-Hammurabi codes should have put primitive bias to rest. The Sumerian Laws of Ur-Nammu provided specific sums to compensate when one cut off the foot of another or injured bone, nose, or tooth. The Akkadian Laws of Eshnunna provided specific sums if one bit and severed the nose of another, injured eye, tooth, or ear, or slapped another. That those laws substantially pre-dated the Covenant Code's talion would contradict rather than support evolutionary theory that talion evidenced primitiveness. Fixed fines of more-ancient texts were rough-and-ready secular justice, only later giving way to Covenant Code eye-for-eye punishment. Indeed the Covenant Code's moral aim invoking talion counteracted widespread practice of treating injury and compensation as acceptable cost, as we would say today of *doing business*. Talion's institution opposed what popular view assumes true that talion replaced even-more savage retaliation. Ancient custom of paying for deliberate harms looked too much like modest toll for the transgressor, the abuse of which talion justice tempered.

Covenant Code eye-for-eye, tooth-for-tooth punishments were also not for adherents to follow literally. No record of proceedings reflects an actual penalty of cutting off foot or hand, or putting out eye. Indeed no record has come to light indicating missing feet, eyes, and hands. Rather, talion admonished that one must not be so careless as to endanger others. The absence among plentiful records of any indication that claimants exacted such punishments reinforces that talion was spur to negotiate over compensation. The Code of Hammurabi had its own talion penalty that a surgeon whose patient dies is to suffer amputated hand. If communities had followed that rule, then Babylonia would have had no surgeons. The message was instead that physicians should take extraordinary care. Given this clear historical data, the modern view that talion represented primitively vengeful and uncompromising Old Testament justice is the perverse view deserving scrutiny.

Consider then what meaning to give talion in its full sacred and historical context. One of the Covenant Code's clearer talion rules, appearing in Deuteronomy 19:16-21, involves malicious witness falsely accusing another of crime, what we today call slander, the oral subset of defamation. Verses 18 and 19 state,

> [I]f the witness proves to be a liar, giving false testimony against his brother, then do to him as he intended to do to his brother. You must purge the evil from among you. The rest of the people will hear of this and be afraid, and never again will such an

evil thing be done among you. Show no pity: life for life, eye for
eye, tooth for tooth, hand for hand, foot for foot.

Note ambiguities in this rule. First, the rule stating to "do to
him as he intended to do to his brother" is not saying directly to
cut off the wrongdoer's hand or foot. If the tort is slander rather
than the intentional cutting off of another's hand, then the *do-to-
him* remedy has nothing to do with cutting off hand. Yet nor
would remedy be to slander back slanderer. Slander victim has
little or no prospect of gaining equivalency, of "purging the evil"
as the rule itself states, through any such remedy. More slander
would only compound harm. What, then, do we make of the life-
for-life, eye-for-eye, tooth-for-tooth remedies? Again note
ambiguity in the text: these phrases contain no verbs. They do
not say to *take* life for life, *put out* eye for eye, or in the given
circumstance, *slander* one who maliciously harms another's
reputation. The rule does not say to take life, eye, tooth, hand,
foot, or reputation of wrongdoer. These implications seem likely,
but of implications we should be wary, especially when
misconstruing sensitive text to be roughly primitive.

Context helps resolve the ambiguity. The period offered
private adjudication within which the injured party held
discretion whether to apply the talion formulae. Ancient historian
Flavius Josephus recorded in Book IV, Section 280, of his *Jewish
Antiquities* that parties settled tort disputes of this kind privately.
Josephus noted that if claimant demanded more than fit injury,
then claimant lost the right of talion altogether. Judicial review so
ensured. Talion merely initiated negotiations between injured
and wrongdoer, as in the Covenant Code's goring-ox provision at
Exodus 21:30 stating, "[I]f, however, the penalty is commuted to a
monetary penalty, he shall pay in redemption of his life whatever
is imposed upon him." Where parties did not agree, court would
commute talion sentence to reasonable monetary penalty. Talion
thus operated much like our own civil-liability system in which as
many as 95% of tort cases resolve voluntarily. Talion remedies
were figures of speech giving the injured claim for full
compensation. Victims had only constrained discretion to require
reasonable compensation. Neither text nor practice mandated
physical retaliation.

Other Old and New Testament verses reinforce this interpretation. Though to the misguided, talion seems to authorize revenge, Proverbs 24:29 cautions claimants not to demand it: "Do not say, 'I will do to him as he has done to me; I will pay the man back for what he has done.'" Restoration, not payback, was talion's intent. Readers could draw similar interpretation from Jesus's admonition in Matthew 5:38-39, "You have heard that it was said, 'An eye for an eye and a tooth for a tooth.' But I say to you, 'Do not resist one who is evil. But if any one strikes you on the right cheek, turn to him the other also.'" Jesus was not changing the law but fulfilling it, that we must settle, not compound differences.

Yet now the argument runs ahead of itself. The point here is that while Babylonians thought themselves ruled by gods of life force (Sin) and practicality (Bel-Marduk), Hebrews knew themselves ruled by the one God (Jehovah), and we rule ourselves under gods of self-realization (Apollos) and materialism (Mammon), each of us, whether ancients or moderns, found necessary similar civil-liability laws, none much more primitive or sensitive than the next. That the earliest of laws involved care for neighbor is no fortuity. The God who required love of neighbor remains the God who, while love itself, still requires love of neighbor. Consider next God's full care expression.

Chapter 4

The Perfect Person

Despite their sensitivity and modernity, ancient tort laws lacked something important that modern tort laws possess. Indeed to state it more accurately, they lacked *someone* who is very much present in tort law today. Ancient tort laws did not expressly and fully reflect the *reasonably prudent person* who provides the foundation for modern tort law. The reasonable person remained inchoate in those ancient laws, hidden until humankind encountered and over centuries gradually came to recognize and fully appreciate the perfect person.

Surely ancient tort laws referred to an external standard of care, as do modern tort laws. For civil liability, communities judge the conduct of one who injures another by *community* rather than individual or subjective standards. When one hurts another, we care not at all for what someone who knew the wrongdoer would have expected from the wrongdoer. An objective standard ignores whether the wrongdoer was habitually sloppy, lazy, inattentive, hurried, hard-hearted, or otherwise careless. For civil liability, we do not through our habits create our own standards of care. Objective standards do not adjust for individual idiosyncrasies. If they did, then they would not be standards at all, never judging anyone responsible to any action other than that which the individual habitually chose. The care standard by which we judge wrongdoer is a general standard of the fittingly careful conduct in the given situation.

To help lawyers, judges, jurors, and litigants understand and apply that community standard, tort law today employs the concept of the ordinarily and reasonably prudent person, what we traditionally knew as the *reasonable man*. Modern tort law invokes the reasonably prudent person to some degree in every negligence claim. Negligence claims are most certainly the driving engine of modern tort and liability-insurance systems. The reasonably prudent person is the focal point around which the tort system decides claims. Standard jury instructions explain negligence to the lay juror in just that way, what the reasonably careful person would or would not do under the circumstances. The reasonable-person standard distinguishes acceptable from unacceptable conduct, meaning conduct out of which legal liability will arise or not arise. The reasonably prudent person is close acquaintance of lawyers and insurance adjusters. Modern tort law would be lost without the theoretically perfect person, one who is never negligent.

Ancient tort laws did not yet state that external standard as the reasonably prudent person. Ancient tort laws established a community standard. One had to make firm boat, guard goring ox horn, repair decrepit wall, and cover pit, whether or not one had personal proclivity to do so. Civil-liability laws required it. Those ancient laws could have held that one must act as would theoretical always-prudent person, but those laws did not state so. They imposed an objective community standard without the concept of the reasonably prudent person. The perfect person did not yet exist even though the condition for existence, in the form of civil liability depending on objective standard, was present, and even though the perfect person's influence operated within that civil-liability system.

Then Jesus Christ came as full embodiment of universal God in human life and form, living with such sacrificially piercing love as expressly to recover from carelessness any who would accept his perfect identity. In the New Testament, Christ's life and teachings formed the canon law that successive popes enforced in western Continental Europe through the first millennium after Christ and well into the second. Channel kept canon law largely out of England, where rulings of Saxon chieftains and kings formed the basis for English common law. Yet Christianity with its intense care standards suffused England, Norman conquerors mixing Roman, canon, feudal, and Frankish laws to establish our progenitor common law. Consider Christ's influence on the common law's recognizing the reasonably prudent person standard.

Today we regard law as such secular institution that we miss how history and culture influence law, which especially excludes sacred influences. Who can judge Christ's influence in bringing into full flower the concept of the reasonably prudent person? We have no direct means to credit Christ for the reasonably prudent person's development in tort law. Yet Christ's influence on spheres outside law was profound. Christian concepts and institutions created modern science's conditions and foundations. Christian morals confirmed family as social order's bedrock. Christ's service ethic became and remains foundation for business, the strength of his promise supporting and facilitating modern commerce. His message to obey properly constituted authority enabled representative government. His unyielding-to-death dissent founded free expression, while his peacefully passionate pursuit of persons founded civil rights. Why would Christian teaching not also affect tort law?

Profound parallels exist between Christ and the reasonably prudent person. Isaiah foretold that Christ would have no beauty or majesty to attract us to him, nothing in his appearance that we would desire. His distinction was not physical, not of standing or place. Christ was born humbly underground without notice except by lowly and alien. He remained unrecognized through youthful life so innocuous that hardly record remains of it. Christ assembled around him ordinary rather than extraordinary or learned followers. His following grew only among the ordinary as he rejected elite invitations, honors, and distinctions. Because he claimed no worldly majesty, Christ lived and taught without notice of nearly everyone of social importance until his last days, when he finally drew perfectly inglorious distinction, murdered by the distinguished on history's single most-awful instrument of public death in shame.

The reasonably prudent person similarly bears no physical majesty or distinction. We expect no great strength, speed, height, or reach of the reasonably prudent person. The reasonably prudent person is not friend of elite. Only the downtrodden injured require his close acquaintance in service of their claims. Distinction would make the reasonably prudent person unfit for that service, making the reasonably prudent person more than ordinary, when ordinariness is what the community standard requires. Distinction would make the reasonably prudent person incapable of relating to the common circumstances in which harm occurs, when so relating is the reasonably prudent person's sole purpose. Like Christ, the reasonably prudent person must relate to the age, sex, height, weight, and other physical characteristics of each of us in our own peculiar circumstance. If the reasonably prudent person were superhuman, then we would have no model for behavior. The reasonably prudent person's utility lies in perfect ordinariness, the only superhuman characteristic perfectly ordinary care in all circumstance.

The reasonably prudent person's anonymity is curious because like the Holy Spirit whom Christ left for us, the perfect person dwells not only in our law but everywhere, wherever two or more gather with duty toward one another. The reasonably prudent person attends every ongoing relationship to which any degree of care is essential. Yet the reasonably prudent person's intimacy does not prevent appearance at every chance encounter of strangers. The reasonably prudent person inhabits every interaction in which any measure of duty exists toward one another, even when strangers on the highway suddenly and unexpectedly meet. Indeed, the reasonably prudent person attends our actions even when we do not gather but instead send abroad our products, services, transactions, and communications, within each of which we regard and treat one another with prudent and ordinary care.

Like Christ, one finds the reasonably prudent person most in evidence among wrongdoers and those whom they injure. The reasonably prudent person appears most plainly where one finds unjustified suffering, where claims arise and litigants invoke, rely on, and dispute the reasonably prudent person's actions and character. The reasonably prudent person compensates and restores the injured while (no less importantly) redeeming the injurer. Yet the reasonably prudent person is also present when no injury occurs, first and primary preventive role to see that no injury occurs, that we comply with care's gentle standard. The reasonably prudent person's presence is proactive, protective, and ameliorative, not merely compensatory, restorative, and redemptive.

Still like Christ, the reasonably prudent person does not seek honor, vaunt power, and take pride in reputation. Among elites, the reasonably prudent person actually has little reputation. Commentators long ago labeled the reasonably prudent person with the denigrating moniker *the odious creature*. Law scholars write and frequently repeat that the reasonably prudent person is inadequate, unmanageable, behind the times, and unsatisfactory, quite a list of pejoratives against one whom we receive solely to call for useful service to the downtrodden injured. Yet like Christ, the reasonably prudent person never forces presence on us. Rather, the reasonably prudent person merely offers service to us to the extent that we find it useful, whether in preventing injury, restoring injured, or redeeming injured.

Commentators even mislabel the reasonably prudent person's care as price to pay for commerce, loss to liberty, and burdensome cost, like spoiled children turning the sweetly mature prudent person into cold-blooded caricature calculating economic formula. Nothing has value exceeding care's value. Yet as with Christ, elites, those who should know him best, accord the reasonably prudent person no such distinction, even though the reasonably prudent person's ordinary standing is necessary, heart and soul dressed in humility for civil liability's service. Nothing in the reasonably prudent person's appearance attracts us because we value his care rather than appearance. If we recognized his humble character and essential purpose, then we would stop our denigration and stop expecting wrong things from him. The reasonably prudent person may then resume and broaden his characteristic work of correcting wrongdoer while restoring those whom wrongdoer injures.

Tort law properly recognizes the reasonably prudent person as the perfect person. Pontius Pilate said of Christ, "I find no fault in him." So too the reasonably prudent person's essential character and constitution is that no fault lies in him. Though one thinks him ordinary in his care, the reasonably prudent person possesses peculiar quality of never having had exhibited less than ordinary care, a claim no other than Christ can make. The reasonably prudent person is in that sense and that sense only an extraordinary man like of whom only once ever walked the earth, in perfectly ordinary perfection. Just as Christ similarly invites us, we turn to the reasonably prudent person for perfectly attainable standard that judge, like Pilate, would also find us free from fault. Moreover, when judged liable for failing in care, we expect the reasonably prudent person, like Christ, to redeem and free us from fault, making us faultless again. The reasonably prudent person is tort law's paradigm person of perfect virtue in and utility for every situation, a person for all ages and seasons.

As the above intimates, the reasonably prudent person is perfect in another important sense that his care standard is always attainable. The reasonably prudent person's perfection is an oddly ordinary and attainable perfection. Like Christ, the reasonably prudent person is perfectly imitable even though superhuman in having none of the faults we know to be so human. The reasonably prudent person is fully human in capability and proportion even though beyond human in being without fault, just as Christ is both human and beyond human to divine. We must be able to attain that which the reasonably prudent person requires of us, or by definition what the reasonably prudent person requires would be neither reasonable nor ordinary. Christ admonished Pharisees for burdening convert with impossible rules, fault that the uninformed today attribute to the reasonably prudent person. The assertion misconceives the reasonably prudent person's nature and obedience required of us. If the reasonably prudent person required the unattainable, something to which not even a saint could conform, then the reasonably prudent person would be at fault and unreasonable, neither of which he can ever be. Prudence is as prudence does, never anything more than the ordinary person can attain.

Some still think the reasonably prudent person a hard taskmaster, just as many have misunderstood Christ to be. The reasonably prudent person's ordinary perfection brings impetuosity out of us, like holding mirror to fitful child. Some misunderstand the reasonably prudent person to deprive us of liberty, making self-fulfillment their libertine god, a law so counter to tort law, one that issues from within themselves to do as they think best for themselves, by ignoring others. The reasonably prudent person, who so easily judges them devoid of care, rankles them by requiring nothing of them other than that they are perfectly capable to perform. The reasonably prudent person has precisely that nature and purpose to mirror carelessness's many small and large imperfections even while revealing his critic's imperfection, just as Christ before Pilate judged the judge who presumed to judge him. The reasonably prudent person makes no claim that we should exhibit more than ordinary care. We must judge the reasonably prudent person by his own character and constitution, not those which his critics incorrectly attribute him.

Far from taskmaster, the reasonably prudent person grants us liberty. Christ's brother James wrote that liberty is to be without fault, loving and caring as Christ did. By acknowledging himself slave to his loving father's will, Christ gained perfect liberty, taking on complete identity of his peculiar man-God self. Those who exhibits Christ's love hardly need to concern themselves with civil liability. They become law unto themselves, offending no one while caring for all, doing as they please at perfect liberty because they choose and exhibit prudence in and toward all. So are the peculiar people who follow Christ, and so are those who follow the reasonably prudent person, complete in their liberty. Care becomes the one activity without limit, against which we face no law. One has perfect liberty within the confines of reasonable prudence, ever-greater freedom to act or not act. Who constrains the reasonably prudent person?

Critics cast the reasonably prudent person's modest constraints as weak check against self-enlarging, self-satisfying liberty, thus making the reasonably prudent person poor minion to an unleashed and supreme liberty. Yet those critics, though published authoritatively in leading journals and cases, hold views that frighten persons of ordinary prudence. Claims that liberty constrains the reasonably prudent person turn sense on its head. The common person in common thought knows that the reasonably prudent person acts at all times unconstrained within sweetly liberating command to care freely but offend enslaved. By constitution and character, the reasonably prudent person authorizes no act or omission other than those for reasonable good of any concerned. The reasonably prudent can in perfect liberty drive in whatever direction for as long as they wish, giving care to fellow travelers along the highways. Law of care is law of perfect liberty. The reasonably prudent person establishes rather than constrains liberty. Ignoring care's freedom, unnatural liberty brought apple to Adam whose careless act Christ redeemed.

Another heavy criticism the reasonably prudent person unfairly bears is that the compensation he commands is mere *transaction cost* or system *inefficiency,* best reduced or eliminated if only things were to work right. The claim is that fees attributed to the reasonably prudent person, and by extension lawyers who retain and employ him to help the injured, are system problems. The claim is that money flowing to the injured is tort law's only arguable good and that fees to the injured person's counsel, those who employ the reasonably prudent person, are inefficiency and loss. Reforms reduce those fees as unwise costs. Alternative no-fault systems eliminate the reasonably prudent person and his wage.

This criticism is at odds with the fundamental role the reasonably prudent person plays. Christ said that worker is worth wage. The reasonably prudent person is in fundamental respect destination alone. Invoking his rule and image on behalf of injured is not merely prelude to compensation but value in itself. Interceding for and counseling the injured has worth independent of monetary recovery. Restoration is not in money but rather what money purchases or represents. The reasonably prudent person's advocacy provides greater lasting benefit than monetary proceeds of that work. Above all, caring for the injured involves advocacy for the injured one's value and cause. That advocacy has enduring value of its own beyond material gain that advocacy may accomplish. The reasonably prudent person's wage represents independent good.

Asserting that fees represent the reasonably prudent person's wages is not word game. Without lawyers trained in the reasonably prudent person's service, few of us could effectively invoke the reasonably prudent person to protect the vulnerable or restore the injured. No wonder that Shakespeare's villain advised first to kill all the lawyers. Lawyers frustrate villainy. They also address and discourage carelessness, which is its own kind of villainy. In the tort system, both plaintiff's and defense counsel invoke the reasonably prudent person. We are the reasonably prudent person's advocates and representatives, though our duties are to clients. When we receive fees, the reasonably prudent person remains present. Without fees to sustain our advocacy, the reasonably prudent person is less in evidence, and so is the independent good his care represents, that fundamental, non-reducible concern of one for another.

Compensation to the injured pays doctors, nurses, therapists, and other health professionals for care that no one would properly label inefficiency or transaction cost. Their care is essential to the injured person's recovery, gain, not a loss. Similarly, compensation for lost wages pays mortgage, car note, and gas bill, and buys food, again for the injured person's care. These interests differ little from the care of the lawyer who provides counsel, answer, solace, hope, and justice, all goods of great value to the injured. The lawyer does not merely invoke the reasonably prudent person to gain monetary recovery to purchase other goods and services. Critics who conceive of lawyers as purely economic agents miss the lawyer's role and function as purveyor of care itself, for soul-healing justice.

Reasonable fees could be flower, not thorn, for care the tort system promotes. Critics who argue otherwise might consider that markets for law services ensure appropriate levels of intercession, service, concern, and advocacy for the most-reasonable price. Where supply of the reasonably prudent person is too small and demand great, wage will rise accordingly, while where supply is great and demand small, wage will fall. Those who possess greater skill at invoking the reasonably prudent person in service of clients receive larger wage while lesser representatives smaller. Do not characterize care's service as cost, when that service is so often balm. The reasonably prudent person is worth these wages.

The powerful despised Christ, as Isaiah foretold hundreds of years earlier, as man of sorrows, familiar with suffering, feet and hands pierced, and clothes stripped and divided among tormenters, and marred beyond likeness. Though he healed thousands with perfect care, love, and wisdom, Christ had no safe place to rest. He instead traveled from town to town, harried, vilified, and finally brutally scourged, cruelly mocked, and crucified for purity in service. None before or since brought same gift only to suffer same brutal humiliation.

Many also scorn the reasonably prudent person. Thousands die violent highway deaths for lack of care, and yet legislatures replace civil liability with statutory no-fault schemes. Thousands more die in hospitals of medical negligence, and yet legislatures and courts limit medical liability. Thousands more did in workplaces, and yet worker's compensation acts limit employer civil liability. Scholars even conclude that tort law should abandon the reasonable-care standard. Public campaigns by commerce chambers and insurance industries, and political campaigns, also scorn the reasonably prudent person. Many now believe his standard of care controlled by special interests. Yet like Christ, the reasonably prudent person knows suffering and sorrow. The carefree who suffer not or little while holding power over others think the reasonably prudent person would restrict that power, in voracious materialism seeing so little of him in their own interests. Only the abased embrace the reasonably prudent person, acutely aware of their need, recognizing their desperate condition. The injured depend on him, unable to provide for themselves. The low places welcome the reasonably prudent person.

The powerful have equal need of the reasonably prudent person. Isaiah foretold that men would pierce Christ and crush him for their own iniquities, punish him to bring us peace, his wounds healing us. Christ predicted his own demise as sacrificial lamb whose blood cleanses us. He made himself the archetype of mythical dying gods and fulfillment of the Old Testament. He was the first and last to both make and complete the claim, bringing alive the idea of one to intercede for us when we injure another. So too does the reasonably prudent person bring peace, order, and restoration out of our conflicts and transgressions. Fault is piercing transgression against the reasonably prudent person. Neither injured nor injurer then hold the standard instead held by the reasonably prudent person without whom we would not even perceive our transgression.

Fortunately, the reasonably prudent person's service does not end at defining transgression. The reasonably prudent person's insult from our transgressions is also our healing. When a wrongdoer's carelessness injures another, the injured is not the only one who requires restoration. Wrongdoers carry guilt of injuring, burdened conscience, and community shame. If a wrongdoer's carelessness did not wound the reasonable person, then wrongdoer would have no redemption from injuring others. Wrongdoer would have neither judgment nor its satisfaction in monetary payment. The reasonably prudent person not only heals injured but also redeems injurer. His insult, meaning recognizing that wrongdoer has violated his standard, begins the wrongdoer's healing. Without the reasonably prudent person's offense, communities could not restore wrongdoers.

We crave and require justification. When Judas brought his awful guilt to Pharisees of betraying innocent Jesus, their response was *who cares?* Cain made similar why-bother-me response millennia earlier when denying that he was his murdered brother's keeper. To ignore guilt is social and spiritual death, completely unsatisfactory in communities of any worthwhile quality. As evidence, Judas's suicide was the effect of the Pharisees' who-cares response. Judas needed forgiveness and redemption in response to his confession but received neither and, crushed by guilt, took his life to end his intolerable condition. Like his mirror reasonably prudent person, Christ instead confronts and redeems guilt, knowing critical value to confession, perceiving possibility of forgiveness, and embodying redemption. To Apostle Paul, Christ was free gift who following our constant transgressions brings justification.

Tort law confronts social, financial, and spiritual responsibility for harm we wreak, providing not only accountability to the injured but also satisfaction of judgment and wrongdoer's forgiveness and redemption. The reasonably prudent person's indispensable role in that critical transaction includes confrontation, confession, judgment, satisfaction, release, and redemption. That process so critical to individual and communal welfare justifies tort law. The care that constitutes and defines the reasonably prudent person and permits his transactions is tort law's ground and foundation. Like Christ, the reasonably prudent person is both justifier and his own justification. The care attribute that defines the reasonably prudent person is unimpeachable and unconditional justifier even of those who have injured. Care is the reasonably prudent person's free gift bringing justification out of transgression. The reasonable person authorizes tort law, as Christ generates social and spiritual life.

Christ's eternity that would ever vanquish him also defines the reasonably prudent person. Although the ancient's overlooked him, the reasonably prudent person has as a concept always existed, just as Christ always existed. As above chapters showed, the reasonably prudent person influenced the earliest laws even if those laws did not expressly recognize him. Traditional views differ. Subsequent chapter shows scholars claiming that tort law gradually developed out of the increasingly refined and articulate reasoning of increasingly enlightened scholars after the Middle Ages. Some writers make that false claim more deliberately than others, tracing tort law origins to the feudal system, claiming that tort law evolved out of the blood feud and medieval rules of vengeance. As evolutionist would have it, primordial reasonably prudent person coalesced out of steaming lake in the Dark Ages to skulk through shoreline mud in medieval England until gaining ground on Renaissance plain, entering as pristine knight in American halls of justice. Yet as the above chapters show, tort law existed millennia earlier. The reasonable person's parents were not medieval England's bewigged jurists. We do ourselves and the reasonably prudent person no credit misapprehending his origin as if it were recent.

Whatever one might say of the reasonably prudent person will not vanquish him. Consideration of others as ends rather than means was Kant's categorical imperative. Tort law's pendulum may swing through generations and ages between more and less care, and with different remedies. Our tort law granting immunity to drunken driver who injures child, reckless employer who kills worker, and defamer ruining reputation, may less reflect the reasonably prudent person's care than the law of our ancestors. Or our tort law may more reflect the reasonably prudent person by allowing claims by injured persons who themselves had degree of negligence. Yet the reasonably prudent person's cause will always prevail because care will always be core to individual and communal welfare. The reasonably prudent person would like our acknowledgment, honor, and advocacy, but the extent to which tort law acknowledges him is not his measure but our measure because he represents the eternal and perfect standard.

Chapter 5

A Code of Care

While Christ embodied the reasonably prudent person as tort law's archetype, tort law on its own spanned the age of his coming. How did tort law do so? An old county courthouse in rural Michigan has three large murals behind the chief judge's bench. The first represents Mosaic law of precedent and tradition, the second natural law written on our hearts after Christ, and third Roman law as positive law of the code. Predating and antedating Christ, the great Roman civil codes contained specific and general tort provisions. Roman code law bridged ancient Hammurabic and Mosaic traditions into early European jurisprudence both English and to a lesser extent French and German that scholars recognize as source for American law. American scholars of earlier generation readily recognized the debt our law owes the Romans, a debt we seldom recognize today in our ahistorical view.

Roman law is not one code but successive codes digesting various customs, distinct from the ancient Jewish laws by its civil rather than criminal and penal form. Money damages and penalties, not death, maiming, or imprisonment, were Roman legal norm. Roman law survived so long in civil form because of power wielded by patriarchal family heads who could when necessary impose private criminal punishments including death. Public courts concerned themselves with monetary penalties for various wrongs one commit against another, much like tort and contract civil liability today.

Roman law's chief historian and proponent Sherman, writing in 1917, divided Roman law into two periods. The first period of local city law was from Rome's founding in 753 B.C. to consolidation of Italy in 89 B.C., so for about 700 years to Christ. The second period of world law lasted until the Roman Empire's demise by Teutonic defeat in Western Europe after Turkish defeat in the east in 1453 A.D. Roman law did not die with the Empire but according to Sherman exerted a profound influence on modern American law. Roman law's general influence likely held true for Roman tort laws particularly because of their number and detail. Sherman lists 30 Roman general tort provisions, 13 more on personal injury, 40 on robbery and theft, 22 on property damage, and 20 on fraud.

Roman codes differed from ancient laws they supplanted. They were more like today's law codes than like ancient recorded traditions, unified broad generally applicable laws to apply in any situation rather than individual case decisions. The Twelve Tables dating to 449 B.C. collected earlier Roman laws. Each Table consisted of several individual statements of law on a particular topic from proceedings preliminary to trial (Table I) to sacral law (Table X) plus two supplementary tables. The longest Table VIII containing 27 statements of law and bearing *Torts* title devoted itself solely to that subject. The Torts Table VIII provided variable, fixed, or double money damages, or physical or capital punishment for, among other things, libel, accidental property damage, personal injury, wrongful death, damage by livestock, cutting trees, theft, usury, and fraud. Table VIII's tenth statement is good example of the crime-like and civil tort remedies:

> If a man willfully set fire to a house, or to a stack of corn set up near a house, he shall be bound, scourged, and burned alive; if the fire rose through accident, that is, through negligence, he shall make compensation, and, if too poor, he shall undergo a moderate punishment.

As a first attempt at codification, the Twelve Tables are curt and rugged contrasted to later Roman tort laws showing greater variety and sensitivity. The millennia-newer Institutes of Justinian dated to 533 A.D. show this more-sensitive later Roman treatment of torts in Institute 4, 1:

Since in the preceding book contractual and quasi contractual obligations have been treated, it remains to treat of obligations arising from tort. And the former, as we have stated in the proper place, are divided into four classes; but the latter are of one class, for all arise from some act, that is from the tort itself, for instance from theft or robbery or damage to property or from injury.

The Institutes of Justinian defined negligence as a distinct concept within a hierarchy and broad array of potential wrongs, examples of which follow:

> And anyone is not liable under this law who kills another man by accident, provided that no negligence exist on his part; for otherwise he is liable under this law for negligence, just as much as for a willful wrongful act. [Institute 4, 3, §3.]

> Want of skill is reckoned as negligence, for instance when a physician has killed your slave by unskillfully operating on him or by giving him a wrong medicine. [Institute 4, 3, §7.]

> Injury in general means anything which is a violation of a legal right; injury in a special sense means sometimes outrage ... sometimes culpable negligence ... as in the Aquilian Law,[] and sometimes iniquity and injustice. [Institute 4, 4, preliminary.]

> An injury is committed not only when anyone is struck with the fist, beaten with clubs, or whipped, but also when anyone suffers abusive language inflicted publicly, or when anyone's property has been taken possession of, as if he were a debtor, by a person who knew that he owed him nothing, or when anyone has written, composed, or published defamatory prose or verse, or has cunningly caused the doing of any of these acts, or when anyone follows a married woman or a boy or girl under the age of puberty, or when some person's chastity is attacked; and indeed it is manifest that injury is committed in many other ways. [Institute 4, 4, §1.]

The sensitivity of Roman tort laws in respects exceeded our own by providing for two different negligence hierarchies. In the first, Roman law divided negligence into three degrees, *lata culpa* or gross negligence, *levis culpa* or ordinary neglect, and *levissima culpa* or slight neglect. In the second, Roman law divided negligence into just two degrees, *culpa levis* or lack of diligence in the applicable trade, and *culpa lata* or neglect of layman's ordinary care. Both schemes explicitly set forth degrees of negligence rather than leaving them to infer, thus holding prospect for wider liability than our tort laws, which we tend to base on negligence of single degree except for gross-negligence liability in some states to overcome governmental immunity and for common carriers for which some states find liability for negligence of slightest degree. We may, in other words, have preserved the Roman's concept of degrees of negligence in certain situations, although scholars debate whether negligence can have anything but single degree.

Roman tort laws worked much like our own tort laws. Roman law distinguished actionable negligence from mere accident without negligence or loss claimant's own fault caused, in both of which cases defendant would not be liable for loss. Digest 19, 2, 25, §7, states, "There is no negligence, if everything is done which a most careful person would do." The Institute of Gaius 3, §211, states, "Damage without the violation of a legal right is not actionable under any law; hence he who without his own negligence or wrongdoing damages another is not liable." Roman tort law both stated or implied that civil liability involved objective reasonableness standard, Digest 4, 2, 6, stating, "Now the fear meant in this Edict is not that felt by a man of weak character, but that which might reasonably happen to a man of very strong character." Digest 50, 17, §203, adopted the equivalent of our own contributory negligence rule, stating, "A person is not injured by what he suffers through his own negligence."

Just as law does today, Roman law clearly distinguished civil tort action from alternative criminal proceeding, in Institute 3, 3, §10, stating: "Finally it must be shown that as to every injury the injured party can have either a civil action or a criminal prosecution." By the Institutes of Justinian in 533 A.D., Roman law had also replaced the Twelve Tables' retributive punishment with monetary compensation:

> Now the penalty for injury in the Law of the Twelve Tables[] was retaliation for a broken limb; but for a mere broken bone money penalties were established indicative of the great poverty of the ancients. But subsequently the Praetors used to allow a person who suffered injury to fix his own estimate, so that the judge would condemn him either for as much as damage estimated by

the injured party, or for a less sum, as seemed right to him. But the penalty for injury provided by the Law of the Twelve Tables has fallen into disuse and that which the Praetor introduced, called honorary,[] prevails in law suits. For the estimate of the injury increases or diminishes according to the rank and dignity of the injury party. [Institutes 4, 4, §7.]

Also, like modern tort rules for damage, Roman tort compensation included not only that for property destruction but for diminution in property's value:

The following has been held, not from the words of the law but by interpretation, that there must be an estimation not only of the value of the thing destroyed ... but also of any damage falling on you though the destruction of the thing, for instance when ... one of a pair of mules or one of a chariot team of four horses has been killed: not only should there be an estimate of the one killed, but also there should be computed how much those which remain have been depreciated. [Institutes 4, 3, §10.]

Roman tort law also included several special rules that modern tort law recognizes. Roman law like today's law provided for vicarious liability of carriers and innkeepers for injury due to fault of unfit employees (Digest 44, 7, 5, §6) and for wrongs of bailees (Digest 4, 9, pr., §1). Roman law like today's law raised the burden of proof for fraud to clear evidence (Code 2, 20, 6). Roman law granted husbands and fathers actions for injury to wife or child (Institute 4, 4, §2), equivalent to modern decisions allowing recovery for loss of consortium or support. Roman law recognized self-defense (Institute 4, 4, §11, and Digest 1, 1, 3), just as law does today. Roman law also like today's law provided specifically for dog-bite liability, modifying negligence rules for application in peculiar circumstance (Digesta 21.1.40, 42).

Earlier commentators traced Roman negligence schemes into English and American decisions, although adopting Roman law depended on its practical value. Beven attributed to Roman law fully one third of an English law treatise from the time of Henry III, when English lawyers still studied Roman law. Roman law's influence was not so much due to Rome's occupation of Britain from 53 B.C. to 410 A.D. but because English law drew from canon law, Roman law's successor influencing laws across

Europe. Roman elements including degrees of negligence became indivisible part of English compendium. Early commentators agreed that Roman and English law were substantially the same as to liability for negligently caused damage. Both systems limited liability for negligent failure to act to only instances involving duty. The Roman *lex Aquilia* made the same distinction English and American law adopted that although the insane are not criminally responsible for act they could not understand would result in harm, they would have civil tort liability. Roman tort law like English law that followed it rejected Mosaic and Talmudic split-the-oxen remedy for goring ox in favor of modern all-or-nothing approach. Roman law held masters vicariously liable for harm their slaves committed just as modern law holds employers vicariously liable. In Digest 9.4.2., §1, and Digest 9.1.1, §§ 4, 5, Roman law held dog owners liable for bites from unrestrained dogs just as law does today. That we now miss the existence and influence of these Roman tort laws is strange.

Roman tort laws may even have influenced England's old laws predating the 1066 A.D. Norman invasion. The oldest surviving laws in Germanic tongue are the Laws of King Ethelbert dated 600 A.D. Those laws indicate that owners of weapons are liable for harm another inflicts using those weapons, although owners can avoid liability on unspecified but presumably exculpatory evidence. Ethelbert, I (Tb.3; L. 3), provides, "if a man furnish weapons to another where there is strife though no evil be done, let him make 'bot' with vi. Shillings." *Bot* was payment for non-lethal injury. Subtly, King Ethelbert's tort law made owner intent more important than infliction of harm, not quite as sensitively as Roman laws before it but still fault-based tort law.

Other hints of tort liability exist during this Dark Age. Another pre-Norman King Ine (688-695 A.D.) had property-damage rule cited as Ine, 42, 49 (Th. 129, 133; L. 106, 110) for "swine that make a habit of helping themselves to unallowed mast and to beasts that break hedges and go in everywhere." This rule also carried with an implication of fault in failing to constrain habitual four-legged wrongdoer. King Alfred (891-901 A.D.) had similar rule fault-based liability rule distinguishing damages for first, second, and third misdeeds of an owner's dog. King Alfred also distinguished damages done by spear properly or improperly carried, another putative negligence rule.

Similarly, in provision cited as Edward the Elder, I. I (Th. 161; L. 141), King Edward (901-25 A.D.) gave to one who injured another opportunity to declare on oath that injury was not "from any knavery, but with full right, without fraud and guilte...," by implication another fault-based rule. More clearly, in a provision cited as Ethelred, 52, embodied in Cnut, II, 69 (Th. 329, 413; L. [§ 68] 258, 354), King Ethelred (980-1016 A.D.) distinguished that "if it be that anyone unwillingly or unintentionally do anything amiss," then "he shall not be like to him who misdoes intentionally and of his own will" because "he who is an involuntary doer of that which he misdoes, he is ever worthy of protection and of the better doom because he was an involuntary doer of that which he did." These fault bases for liability likely did not arise independent of but were likely influenced by widely published Roman and canon tort laws.

Clearest example of graduated fault-based pre-Norman tort law comes from the Winchester Code of King Cnut (1027-34 A.D.). In one law dealing with use of and control over one's weapons, the Winchester Code distinguished among intentional conspiratorial wrong, negligent wrong, and innocent act:

> § 76. And I hold it right, though any one set his own spear at the door of another man's house, and he have an errand therein; or if any one quietly lay any other weapon, where they would be still if they might; and any man then seize the weapon and do any harm therewith; then it is right that he who wrought that harm, also make 'bot' for the harm. And he who owns the weapon, let him clear himself, if he dare, [by swearing] that it never was either by his will, or in his control, or by his counsel, or with his cognizance: then it is God's law, that he be innocent; and let the other who wrought the deed, see that he make 'bot' as the law may teach.

The Winchester Code's cautious enumeration of fault-based circumstances where weapon owner's liability might arise shows the lawgiver's aversion to liability without fault. The Code rests liability on proof of an intentional tort that injury be "by his will" or "by his counsel," then on proof of negligence that injury is "in his control" or "with his cognizance." Though modern language would have differed, opinion writer today could hardly have been more sensitive in setting forth circumstances where liability for misuse of one's weapon should accrue.

Thus review of ancient sources shows that today's tort law includes features similar to ancient tort law. Tort law today has similar negligence, strict liability, and intentional tort themes seen in ancient laws, direct and vicarious liability, and contributory negligence. Parallels also exist to ancient tort law anomalies. Today's tort law presumes damage or limits recovery for specific injuries just as ancient law did. Worker's compensation specific-loss provisions set fixed amounts for loss of finger, hand, arm, foot, or leg, as some ancient tort laws did. Damages caps limit amounts awarded, while minimum statutory amounts for motor-vehicle insurance policy limits set recovery floors. Looking critically at our own statutes and schedules makes harder sniffing disdainfully at arbitrariness in ancient fixed-compensation rules. Just as ancient law permitted the injured party to demand compensation but failing voluntary settlement left determination to independent tribunal (Exodus 21:22 is an example), so too practice today allows claimant demand and party negotiation but independent tribunal determination. Many ancient tort laws are substantially our own.

We can learn from ancient tort laws. Writing in the Harvard Law Review nearly 100 years ago, Isaacs cautioned against assuming either an early golden age of tort law or the opposite that ancient laws magnified defects present in early English laws. Simply because some law in early English Year Books appears crude or amoral does not mean that earlier Anglo-Saxon laws were devoid of morals. To extrapolate too far from incipient trend is classic error for historian as much as for laboratory scientist. The same caution applies to moderns making modest adjustment in liability laws to fit new technologies. We should not construe such adjustments as evidence of our higher moral development or tort law's historical march. Isaacs saw both upward movement toward clearer morality and downward movement away from humanity's inherent value in tort law's attempts to classify conduct to meet society's complex ethical demands. We should

89

not see our adjustments of tort law as either abandoning or reaching ideals but rather as recognizing old limitations in new technological circumstance. In all ages, law constantly approaches but fails to quite meet its ethical imperative.

Sensitive rules of ordinary care existed from our earliest legal texts. Care always has been universal imperative that law must accommodate and express in tort-like system. Care existed as tort law's root then and exists as root now. Negligence is simply absence of care essential to meaningful society. With care as timeless essential, we should not speculate that the law of care developed in evolutionary model from primitive to profound across the ages. Instead, simply observe how tort law reflected universal imperative from society to society that we care for one another in sufficient degree to make life reasonably safe, ordered, and meaningful. Care has not changed, nor has social imperative that laws administer it. Ancient texts show when fairly read that we are no more moral today in conceiving of and administering tort law and in how those laws reflect care than were the ancients. Indeed aspects of ancient tort laws emphasize care beyond that which some tort laws reflect today. The history of tort law is surely not its recent emergence. We value mobility so highly today that thousands die and suffer serious injury on highways regulated by no-fault tort laws making care little or no factor. Care has the same role today that it did for those recording and applying ancient tort laws, to ensure that laws adequately reflect care even in hazardous circumstance. Care's imperative existed from the beginning in earliest recorded law and continues through ancient and medieval times to modernity.

Chapter 6

A Natural Law

How then did this fundamental law of love cross the divide from ancient and medieval to modern? American legal scholars could responsibly begin law's historical and conceptual analyses with the Declaration of Independence, which rooted American law and government. American law rests on the Declaration as origin of self-government. The U.S. Constitution and law flowing from it — not merely structure of government but also enumeration of rights — depend on the Declaration. Yet we owe the Declaration of Independence more than the fact of law and government. The Declaration also eloquently states natural, commonly held, and fundamental principles for law and government.

Tort law, as a foundation of the justice system that the Constitution preserves and provided for, also has its historical and conceptual bases in the Declaration of Independence. What does the Declaration tell us about tort law? Nothing directly, indeed as it says little or nothing directly about criminal law, property law, contract law, or other legal fields. Yet indirectly, revealing the natural basis for law and government, the Declaration also tells us much about all forms of law including tort law. The Declaration includes several key phrases and an overall design that give us fresh understanding of tort law's basis.

The Declaration begins with an important preamble followed by a list of grievances against the former law-giver England's King George. The first of those grievances is that the king had "refused his Assent to Laws, the most wholesome and necessary for the public good." Law is necessary. The absence of law means chaos and tyranny. Laws though must be wholesome, made for public good. Other Declaration grievances include: government was not representative; government was not constituted to protect against external attack and internal foment; enough judges had not been designated, and those who were depended on the king's will; immigration and migration was unduly restricted; the military was not subject to civilian power; jury trial had not been assured; and colonists had been forced to become executioners against themselves.

The Declaration's list of grievances served important political function in rallying the American populace and committing their leaders to independence's cause. Yet that list serves more long-lasting function defining proper nature and contours of government. The grievances readily established that laws must be both reasoned and representative. Law not representative of the interests of those whom it governs has no mandate, lacking consent of the governed. Laws that are inequitable to the governed or laws lacking in sound reason are not laws but instead whimsical or tyrannous edicts. The Declaration binds office holders to circumspect levels of reason and representation. In its list of grievances, the Declaration imposes fundamental obligations on government officeholders including those who make or modify tort law.

Key phrases in the Declaration's preamble include that Americans possess "certain inalienable rights" granted them by their "Creator," and that the new nation must accordingly be governed by "the Laws of Nature and of Nature's God." By referring to the Creator and to God, the Declaration did not intend that the new government be a theocracy. The founders' writings make obvious that conclusion, as do their varied religious denominations, governance within their several states, and their subsequent adoption of the First Amendment's Disestablishment Clause. Yet by referring to Creator-endowed inalienable rights, and to Laws of Nature and of Nature's God, the founders exhibited theistic philosophy of government. While the Declaration did not establish a theocracy, the Declaration also did not mean that the new nation would be governed by deterministic and materialist laws assuming absence of Creator. The founders were not thinking of the Laws of Nature in the way that readers today may think of *mother nature*. Rather, the Laws of Nature and Laws of God carried specific meaning for the founders, reflected in the Declaration's first grievance that laws are necessary and must be wholesome. The Laws of Nature represented theistic philosophy of reason today carrying the label *natural law*.

United States Supreme Court Justice Joseph Story makes the most-interesting figure confirming natural law's influence on American jurisprudence. Justice Story was born in Massachusetts in 1779, just after the Declaration. His father was one of the revolutionists disguised as an Indian who famously poured British tea into Boston Harbor, and who later served under General George Washington as surgeon for revolutionary forces. After taking a degree at Harvard College, Justice Story was several times elected and re-elected Salem's representative to the Massachusetts legislature (he also served one session in the United States Congress during this period), up until 1811 when President James Madison appointed him justice of the United States Supreme Court. He was just 32 years old when appointed to the high Court. Nearly three decades after Justice Story was appointed to the new nation's high Court, he received in 1829 a chaired professorship at Harvard Law School.

Justice Story shows us how the Declaration of Independence became bridge across which natural law passed from its scholar authors Grotius and Pufendorf into the soul of American law. Justice Story followed the tradition of addressing the Harvard Law faculty when he received his professorship. In that address, titled *The Value and Importance of Legal Studies*, Justice Story disclosed that Harvard hired him to teach the Law of Nature, as well as the Law of Nations (international law), Maritime and Commercial Law, Equity, and Constitutional Law. As to his first subject the Law of Nature, that which the Declaration of Independence had said would govern the new nation, Justice Story acknowledged that this law "lies at the foundation of all other laws, and constitutes the first step in the science of jurisprudence." Justice Story then defined the Law of Nature as "nothing more than those rules which human reason deduces from the various relations of man, to form his character, and regulate his conduct, and thereby insure his permanent happiness." Natural law looks to man's "duties to God, his duties to himself, and his duties to his fellow men; deducing from those duties a corresponding obligation." Natural laws are those laws reason deduces as fitting and necessary, from consideration of man's nature. One could not have clearer confirmation than Justice Story's Harvard appointment and address that the Declaration, the nation, and its still-new high Court made natural law the foundation of American government.

Justice Story did not stop there in his 1829 Harvard address but also gave natural law Christian imprimatur and foundation. "With us, indeed, who form a part of the Christian community of nations, the law of nature has a higher sanction," he continued in his Harvard address, "as it stands supported and illustrated by revelation." "Christianity," Justice Story went on, coincident with natural law, "has added strength and dignity to the latter by its positive declarations." "It unfolds our duties with far more clearness and perfection than had been known before its promulgation; and has given a commanding force to those of imperfect obligation." Not only that, "It seems to concentrate all morality in the simple precept of love to God and love to man," while at the same time, "It points out the original equality of all mankind in the eyes of the Supreme Being...." Ultimately, "by unfolding, in a more authoritative manner, the doctrine of the immortality of the soul, it connects all the motives and actions of man in his present state with his future interminable destiny." "It teaches him that the present life is but the dawn of being; and that in the endless progress of things the slightest movement here may communicate an impulse which may be felt through eternity." The Declaration's theistic grounding elevated America's natural law.

Natural law joined fundamentals like truth, public goods, private rights, fitness and fairness, equity and proportion, and above all reason with material, practical, and pragmatic concerns. Natural law involved social science, using observation to deduce first principles that lawmakers could use to shape subject behavior for the greatest benefit. The Declaration's reference to the Laws of Nature and of Nature's God intended that the new government would promulgate natural laws. Its references are unmistakable that the new government would treat the governed as Creator creations under laws fitting to that created nature. This much of the Declaration suggests sound basis for American laws promoting public good based on experience of human nature. The Declaration did not though have anything direct to say about tort law.

What though did the natural law scholars on whom the founders relied say about tort law? The founders relied on the thinking and writing of John Locke, Thomas Hobbes, and David Hume as well as earlier natural law scholars Hugo Grotius and Samuel Pufendorf. Grotius and Pufendorf were first to develop the natural law school of thought on which Locke and Hobbes built and that then made its way into the Declaration of Independence, even though scholars trace natural law back through Aquinas and Augustine to Aristotle. While the Declaration did not cite these thinkers, its authors derived portions of its natural law references from them. Grotius and Pufendorf each elaborated the natural law basis for tort law. Both Grotius and Pufendorf articulated that basis largely where it lies today, in natural responsibility for harm caused by fault, neglect, or negligence, as breach of duty of that ordinary care so fitting to human nature and relations.

Following chapters show again that the fact that these two eminent 17th-century law writers Grotius and Pufendorf each clearly articulated the fault basis for tort law contradicts today's generally accepted wisdom. Law schools teach that the fault basis for tort law developed later than the 17th century. The above chapters show that it most certainly did not. Negligence liability providing for compensatory damages has been around since earliest known laws. Yet the natural law writings of Grotius and Pufendorf show indisputably that negligence liability was already in their day known and the preferred form of legal recourse. Law scholars articulated fault-based, natural law foundations for tort law long before the Declaration of Independence incorporated natural rights, as the following brief discussion shows.

Dutch playwright, poet, and legal scholar Hugo Grotius lived from 1583 to 1645. Scholars today credit him with originating the *social-contract* theory of the state within the natural law school. Social-contract theory posited that states gain their authority from the consent of those whom they govern, in social compact or agreement. The Declaration of Independence and United States Constitution are prime examples. Yet Grotius's natural law had more than simply that to do with tort law. Grotius conceived of law as deduced by human reason nearly like mathematicians deduce formulas that other mathematicians must on their face accept as sound and reliable. Two plus two always equals four. So too from human consciousness and rationality may we deduce certain laws governing behavior. In founding law in reason, Grotius either divorced law from divinity or recognized rational nature of divine. Either way, Grotius's natural philosophy departed from his age's prevailing scholasticism that Augustine and Aquinas handed down through the ages.

Grotius stated the natural basis of tort law in his 1625 work *On the Law of War and Peace*. In Book I, Chapter 3, Part vi, Grotius specifically addressed the "methods in law to prevent intended injuries, as well as actions for those actually committed." In addressing his work to tort law, Grotius first recognized that Aristotle in the fourth book of his *Politics*, Plato in his ninth book on laws, and Homer had each already addressed redress of personal injuries through civil damages action. Civil liability was nothing new to Grotius. Grotius then discussed in Book II, Chapter 17, the "[d]amages occasioned by injury, and the obligation to repair them," that is, "the rights resulting to us from injuries received." Grotius simultaneously indicated that he was addressing not merely events arising from contract relationship but moreover "every act of commission or neglect repugnant to the duties required of all men, either from their common nature or particular calling."

Grotius then cited compensation law's ordinary basis, "For such offences naturally create an obligation to repair the loss or injury that has been sustained." That natural obligation subsists in that "God has given life to man, not to destroy, but to preserve it; assigning to him for this purpose a right to the free enjoyment of personal liberty, reputation, and the controul over his own actions." Grotius's reference to divinity was not authoritative or revelatory because in its workings natural law depends on neither. Grotius was not a scholastic like Aquinas. Rather, Grotius was simply stating what anyone can readily observe, that humans, created as both living and sentient of that life, hold inherent volition not only to enjoy that life but, as natural consequence of that right, also duty to respect life and enjoyment of others. From the simply rationality of his writing, treating Grotius not as historical figure but as contemporary figure would seem natural enough, which is exactly the point that tort law to Grotius was natural outgrowth of fundamental truths we must acknowledge about our condition.

Grotius's writings about tort law show little mystery. He knew precisely where to rest the duty that we owe one another, which is on our ability by our own conduct to injure one another. Grotius rested tort law's "obligation to repair the losses suffered by negligence" either on "that duty aris[ing] from law" or on the "peculiar office" or "capacity" that tortfeasor held toward the injured. Capacity to harm creates corresponding duty not to harm. By this equating, Grotius meant that the tortfeasor "is bound by that right, which strict justice requires, whether that duty arises from law, or from the capacity, which the person bears." Grotius held that this duty to control one's own actions so as not to injure another extended to the point that "every subject has a right to require it" at least "where the law expressly declares or evidently implies that certain acts shall be performed." These formulations are sufficiently similar to our own conceptions of tort law duties arising either by law or relationship as to regard as thoroughly modern.

Grotius envisioned no utopia. He did not permit this duty of care to impose upon people an affirmative duty to do everything beneficial and good for one another, absent express or implied legal obligation. Rather, "the bare circumstances of an action being fit or proper" does not demand its performance, "nor does the neglect of it entitle the party suffering to any legal redress. Because it does not follow that a thing must belong to a person [simply] because it is fit or beneficial for him." Citing Aristotle and Cicero, Grotius accepted that, short of violating this duty not to injure, the law should permit people "to do what they like, rather than what they ought to do" for one another. Grotius ended Book II, Chapter 17, with the caution that, when the only omitted duty was one of charity, "there can be no redress for such omission," because "every legal remedy must be founded on some peculiar right."

On the other hand, Grotius readily extended fault-based tort liability, as we do today, to partners and principals who enjoyed vicariously the benefit of negligent actions their agents undertook. Earlier in Book II, Chapter 17, Grotius wrote, "But besides the person immediately doing an injury, others may be bound also to repair the losses of the suffering party. For as a person may be guilty of offences by negligence as well as by the commission of certain acts, so they may be done also by accessories, as well as principals." Grotius's definition for a principal may have been somewhat different than we use today, but not that different: "Now a principal in any crime or offence is one, that urges to the commission of it, that gives all possible consent, that aids, abets, or in any shape is a partner in the perpetration of it."

Thus Grotius's treatment of tort law was not by mere passing reference but instead integral to his study of law as a whole. To Grotius, tort law was neither vestigial nor developing appendage to law but part of the body of law itself. Insofar as the founders who wrote the Declaration of Independence had a working knowledge of Grotius, and shared his natural law views, they would also have had an appreciation for the centrality of tort law. Because Grotius in the 17th century had a very clear and suitably modern understanding of fault-based tort law based on natural law principles, so would the authors of the Declaration of Independence.

Grotius was not the only writer of his age to articulate natural basis for tort law. Samuel Pufendorf also did so in his 1673 work *On the Duty of Man and Citizen According to Natural Law*. One can hardly mention Grotius without also Pufendorf, although they shared nothing in time, place, or circumstance. Pufendorf, a German legal scholar writing 50 years after the Dutchman

Grotius, built on Grotius's natural law writings. Pufendorf was first to hold university chair in natural law. That distinction alone suggests that Pufendorf was first to bring natural law into jurisprudence mainstream, even placing it at fore. Under the modernizing influence first of Grotius and then of Pufendorf, Roman law and the scholasticism, canon law, and papal law that followed it gradually gave way to the natural law that was foundation for the Declaration of Independence. American jurisprudence is not Roman jurisprudence, nor particularly scholastic or canon law, even though we see hints of their influence. For the most part, and despite influence of modern realists, materialists, and relativists, American jurisprudence is the natural law jurisprudence of Pufendorf.

Pufendorf specifically addressed his writing to the natural basis for fault, or negligence, as the underpinning of tort law. Pufendorf did so by beginning his discussion in Chapter II, Part 17, of *On the Duty of Man and Citizen*, with intentional or "premeditated" injuries. He then considered instances without premeditated intent where "harming another is called an accident or a fault, more or less serious, according to the seriousness of the thoughtlessness and neglect, in consequence of which the encounter occurred." Pufendorf recognized immediately that injuries occurred either accidentally with no fault or resulting from fault. Then in short paragraph immediately following this introduction of the law of fault or negligence, Pufendorf explained again what thinkers meant by natural law:

> With respect to its author, the law is divided into divine and human, the one enacted by God, the other by men. But if law be considered according as it has a necessary and universal adaptation to men or not, it is divided into the natural and the positive. The former [natural law] is so adapted to the rational and social nature of man, that an honorable and peaceful society cannot exist for mankind without it. Consequently it can be investigated and learned as a whole, by the light of man's inborn reason and a consideration of human nature. The latter kind of justice by no means flows from the common condition of human nature, but proceeds from the decision of the lawgiver alone. And yet it ought not to lack its own reason, and the utility which it effects for certain men or a particular society. But while the divine

law is now natural and now positive, human law is, in the strict sense, altogether positive.

Pufendorf linked tort law so closely to natural law because reason, reasonableness, and reasonable care are foundation for both law generally and tort law specifically. To Pufendorf as to other natural-law thinkers, reason must deduce from what we know and experience of human nature, laws necessary to peace and order. As Pufendorf wrote in Chapter III, Part 11, "The nature of man is so constituted that the race cannot be preserved without the social life, and man's mind is found to be capable of all the notions which serve that end."

Pufendorf returned in Chapter VI titled "Mutual Duties, and First, That of Not Injuring Others" to natural basis for tort law. Pufendorf first distinguished general duty of all persons toward one another, owed from fact of our creation as social creatures, from specific duties that arise either from dealings or the status of individual persons. Tort law follows the same distinction today in recognizing both general duties and specific duties within certain relationships or by status. An example is that although one may have no general duty to repair someone else's premises, negligently performing contractual repair may give rise to an action for resulting injury. You would not sue just anyone for injury caused by defective stair but might sue contractor whose negligence created the defect. Similarly, you would not sue a passerby for failing to give first aid in an emergency. Law would not permit you to do so. Yet you might sue the emergency personnel who, called to the scene, provided such incompetent aid as to cause further injury.

Pufendorf then stated in Chapter VI, Part 2, maxim that, "Among the absolute duties, i.e., of anybody to anybody, the first place belongs to this one: let no one injure another." Pufendorf did not conceive this duty as literally absolute, in the manner stated. Rather, he qualified the duty in several respects including by right of self-defense. Yet he first set forth in Chapter VI, Part 4, civil recourse that we expect of tort law:

> It follows also that, if a man has been hurt by another, or a loss inflicted in any way that can be properly laid to the other's charge,

it must so far as possible be made good by him. For otherwise it would be a vain injunction, not to injure, or not to inflict loss, if the man who has actually been injured must swallow his loss, and his assailant can in security, and without refunding, enjoy the profit of the wrong he has done. For human depravity will never refrain from mutual injuries, unless there is the necessity of restitution. And it would be difficult for the man who has suffered loss to make up his mind to live at peace with the other, so long as he did not obtain reparation from him.

After articulating in Chapter VI, Parts 7 and 8, vicarious liability arising from injuries caused through principal-agent and joint-venture relationships (another indication of depth with which he treated tort law), Pufendorf returned to fault basis for civil duty to make good for another's injury. It is "[n]ot alone," Pufendorf wrote in Chapter VI, Part 9, "the man who has injured another with malice aforethought" who "is bound to make good the" injury or loss. Rather, one must make good the injury is "also he who, without direct intention, has done so through neglect, or a fault which it was easy to avoid." Modern readers might not be comfortable with Pufendorf's "easy to avoid" definition for neglect or fault. We today equate "ease" with something less than the ordinary effort required for reasonable care. Yet Pufendorf's meaning is that duty to compensate for harm rests on proof that actor could with reasonable effort have avoided harm. Again, Pufendorf rested that duty on "sociability" of human nature that, together with human self-interest, imposes duty "to act so circumspectly that our intercourse does not become formidable or insufferable to others." Modern readers would accept Pufendorf's *circumspection* as equivalent to modern tort law's ordinary care.

For any who remain unconvinced that Pufendorf articulated then what we today recognize as the ordinary-care standard, he then immediately elaborated upon what other (higher or lower) standards of care should exist in special circumstances, which happen to be modified duties tort law today also recognizes:

> And then, in consequence of a particular obligation, one is often required to use extraordinary diligence. In fact even the slightest fault can suffice to require restitution, provided the nature of the matter does not actually resent, as it were, the most exact diligence; or if the blame does not belong rather to the man who

suffers the damage, than to him who causes it; or unless great excitement, or the circumstances of the case, do not admit a studied circumspection; for example, if one, while brandishing his arms in the heat of battle, should injure a man standing near him.

A "particular obligation," like physician agreement to treat patient or contractor's agreement to repair, may impose "extraordinary diligence." On the other hand, the heat of battle may excuse any but the grossest indifference. Note also Pufendorf's reference in the quote immediately above to instances where "blame" would "belong rather to the man who suffers the damage, than to him who causes it," in which cases Pufendorf would excuse or minimize liability. Though he left the reference unelaborated, what Pufendorf wrote suggests to modern reader present tort defenses of contributory or comparative negligence. We do not hold another liable for injury to ourselves that is our own fault. Indeed Pufendorf immediately clarified in Chapter VI, Part 10, that no liability existed without fault:

> But whoever injures by mere chance, and without his own fault is not bound to make restitution. For nothing having been committed which can be laid to the man's charge, there is no reason why the unwilling agent should atone for an evil that was destined to happen, rather than the other, who has suffered it.

Thus as early as the 1600s, at modern jurisprudence's dawn, writings of Grotius and Pufendorf articulated natural basis for tort law. Current scholars and generations before them have set aside these gems of natural law, notwithstanding that the writers of the Declaration of Independence and the Constitution made them explicit basis for American law. The critical school of Oliver Wendell Holmes and Christopher Columbus Langdell would before long undermine confidence in the Declaration's natural law doctrine that Justice Story had so celebrated at Harvard. Pragmatic utilitarianism would become rule among scholars. Yet against the mechanistic harshness of some modern tort-law regimes, fault-based natural law still seems secure harbor for sensitive reason and responsible external standard. Scholars promoting alternative regimes should admit natural basis for tort law, stated in writings well known to those who founded and formed our government. The Declaration of Independence brought tort law's natural roots and long history into modern American jurisprudence.

Chapter 7

Attributes of Care

It seems appropriate here to take a closer look at this strangely timeless imperative of care before exploring how the law has come to treat it in modern and post-modern eras. What exactly does law mean when saying that one person owes care to another? We see plenty of care exercised in the hands of a fine surgeon treating an accident victim, skilled pilot landing an airliner in a storm, well-versed engineer designing a building's structure and foundation, or nurse attending an elderly patient back to independent health. Yet how does law define care? We must answer that question before taking on current critics who say that care exists only as imagination's figment within whatever cultural and linguistic construct we make of it.

The care at the heart of tort law's ancient civil duty deserves clearer definition from lawyers who advocate and guard it, who wring compensation for clients and make their living from it. We practice a law of love without knowing its full meaning. Because care occupies a central place justifying tort law as essential to ordered liberty, care deserves greater attention in instructing law students, selecting and advocating tort cases, judicial and legislative shaping of tort law, and instructing juries. We teach torts, argue tort cases to juries, and reform tort law without adequate understanding of what it means for one person to show reasonable care for another. At tort law's center is an enormously powerful enigma, this timeless standard of reasonableness.

Other disciplines study care. Physiotherapists find care's meaning in enabling and maximizing of patients wellbeing.

105

Pharmacists see in care its empathy, support, compassion, protection, trust, cooperation, and education. Nurses recognize care as important universal form of human expression. Decades ago, Jean Watson redefined nursing as the science of caring and made a career of studying the meaning of care, to reduce ambiguity and reinvigorate the profession. That profession today recognizes Watson's ground-breaking exposition of ten *carative factors* as nursing's dominant model. Nurses define care as interpersonal satisfying of human needs, promoting growth and health, and preserving self-determination especially for the suffering and weakened. Even among modern procedural demands and specialization, nurses still structure their profession around care's sensitive altruistic value system, their goal to instill hope through supportive relationships based on problem solving and education, grounded on the universals of kindness, concern, and love for others. Some professions still understand the value of attending to care as the core enlivening value.

Why not lawyers? Law commentators write little about the attributes of care. Some have made brief attempts to describe few characteristics of the reasonably prudent person. Half a century ago commentator James listed judgment, knowledge and experience, perception of risk, skill, and sanity as the reasonable man's attributes. A few years later, the American Law Institute's Restatement (Second) of Torts §283, Comment b, included "qualities of attention, knowledge, intelligence, and judgment" among care's attributes. More recently, treatise-writer Dobbs listed the reasonably prudent person's intelligence, perception, memory, and knowledge. Commentator Feldman sees in care virtues of reasonableness, prudence, and carefulness. Yet right where tort-law study might profitably focus on these and other attributes of care, legal writings lack definite study of care.

As a result, juries have little guidance in negligence cases on what constitutes care. Most pattern jury instructions use the concepts of ordinary care and the reasonably prudent person. Yet jury instructions on those concepts are murky, leaving hidden deeper meaning of the reasonable-person standard. Instructions refer to standards without clue on the standards' nature, source, or contours. Even linguists and social scientists who propose

106

revising pattern jury instructions have done so not to further define care but rather to simplify negligence language. Jurors are not the only ones left guessing. Commentators search for descriptive theory, offering and employing the reasonable-care standard without defining or perhaps even believing in it. Indeed, commentators label the reasonably prudent person "odious" while others fashionably denigrate care as little more than empty vessel.

Lawyers and judges managing civil-liability litigation should know how law defines care and its antithesis carelessness, given that tort cases rest on the premise of wrongdoer fault. We should know what carelessness looks like in its common expression and characteristics. To know attributes of carelessness should have value to tort practitioners to whom carelessness is practice's lifeblood. To know wrongful death, personal injury, property damage, and even fraud and defamation, one must understand carelessness. If we knew common and essential attributes of carelessness, then we might better counsel clients, select and advocate their cases, teach law students, and decide tort cases. Yet modern legal philosophy tends to hide rather than promote understanding of care and its indispensable role contributing to ordered liberty. When scholars label care to be spurious, we lose rather than harness its power. Care measures us and our age more than we measure it. The extent to which tort law recognizes, invokes, and promotes care measures how just we are, just as it has measured the justice of prior societies and generations.

The attributes within the duty of care prefigure acts of care that flow from the duty. Law permits lay juries to decide complex and technical liability issues involving airline crashes, products liability, medical malpractice, and other tort cases precisely because we believe that jurors can still reliably reduce those complex issues to how the involved actors valued or failed to value the lives in their care as against their own interests. We trust juries to decide because the care basis for decision is so rich, common, and accessible.

Care's attributes are distinct from careful acts. Acts evidence care, for instance the deftness with which surgeon wields scalpel.

Yet acts do not define care. Rather, motivating commitments, attitudes, and intentions define care. Deft scalpel demonstrates nothing of care when wielded on wrong limb or in unnecessary surgery motivated by financial gain. Care begins with will that motivates resulting act. We judge a vehicle driver speeding along a highway differently depending on whether for pleasure of speed or to deliver injured patient to hospital. Care often means driving slowly but sometimes the opposite driving fast, as when entering a freeway. We judge care on attitude, intent, motivation, and willing, using acts only as care's evidence while locating care in how one regards another. The attributes of the reasonable person of care justifies and grounds tort law.

Attributes of care and carelessness both inform and organize our understanding of tort law. Those attributes are what tort texts teach, judges judge, and tort practitioners practice implicitly. We conceive of tort law as disjointed body of rules without organizing principles, when to the contrary the attribute of care are organizing principles whether or not adequately studied and expressed. Manufacturing generates products liability, publishing generates defamation, professional service malpractice, and other social conduct other liability, under tort rules and doctrines because of the latent dictates of care, even if we do not acknowledge the existence and imperative of those dictates. Consider then the following table listing attributes of care and carelessness, first in their commonality, then in their opposition.

TABLE

	Attributes of Care	Attributes of Carelessness
Shared:	Willing (volition)	Willing
	Perception (knowledge)	Perception
	Effectiveness (efficacy)	Effectiveness
	Liberty	Liberty
Opposed:	Impartiality	Partiality (prejudice)
	Humility (condescension)	Pride
	Mercy (leniency)	Vengeance
	Judgment (justice)	Arbitrariness (injustice)
	Truth (authenticity)	Falsity
	Unselfishness	Selfishness
	Discipline (self-control)	Indulgence
	Reason (rationality)	Irrationality

Virtue (disposed to good)	Opposition to good
Compassion	Cruelty
Proportionality	Disproportion

Consider the first attribute that care must be willing, voluntary or volitional. Law would be nonsense to require something of someone that the person is not capable to choose or not choose. Law does not operate on automatons but on the will of humans. Willing or volition is cardinal attribute of tort law's care. "There can not be an act without volition," the Restatement (Second) of Torts §2, comment a, declares it. We do not consider one to be careful without first concluding that the person had choice. To consider one *careful* simply because they caused no injury would be nonsense if they had no capacity to injure and so no choice, willing, or volition in not causing injury. Care implies choosing. Choice is the litigant's great tool, defining tort claims like no other care attributes. When a defendant can legitimately ask, "But what could I have done to avoid injury?" and the answer is "Nothing," then liability will not exist. When by contrast plaintiff demonstrates that defendant had but eschewed reasonable alternative that would have prevented plaintiff's harm, we know what care looks like.

Tort rules and doctrines express volition as care's attribute. Very young children have no liability for unconsidered instinctive acts that cause harm, lacking will and volition for well-being of others. Tort rules also excuse the very aged and infirm who lack the capacity to act voluntarily. We find similar non-liability absent volition, where injury results from lack of ordinary physical capacity such as blindness or paralysis. Act of God cases likewise excuse liability for unforeseen harm relating to catastrophic natural events, where defendant had no volition in the matter. Tort law even excuses harm due to defendant's sudden waking, epileptic seizures, or involuntary intoxication, absent volition. The American Law Institute's Restatement (First) of Torts § 14 holds that "external manifestation of the will is necessary to constitute an act and an act is necessary to make one liable...."

Care also requires perception, knowledge, or intelligence sufficient to perceive the risks that our actions create to others. Care implies not only volition but also knowledge or perception of the choice. One cannot meaningfully choose to act with care without knowing the risks the choice implicates. Persons sometimes act innocent of knowledge of the risks they create. Children do hazardous things for lack of perception. Drug makers may sell diethylstilbestrol without the ability to know that it will injure the user's children and grandchildren. Knowledge is a necessary attribute of care because responsibility for care cannot arise without ability to know what care requires. Care thus also has an aspect of virtue, meaning the disposition to choose the beneficial rather than harmful. Knowledge alone of risk is not enough for care if the knowing actor instead chooses the harmful. Care implicates the desire to conform one's conduct to minimize risk. Knowing risks, we must engage our conscience to pursue risk-reducing conduct. From care's perspective, intelligence exists not to do harm or for self-expression but to promote well-being of ourselves and others. Ordinary perception combined with desire to pursue good is care's prime attributes without which we would all perish.

Tort rules and doctrines express intelligence as care's attribute. Duty depends on the knowledge and sophistication expected of the actors. In treating patients, tort law expects physician interns to exercise a physician's skill, knowledge, and training, not merely those of a just-graduated medical student. Tort law requires pilots to exercise the skill, knowledge, and training of reasonably prudent pilots, not of just anyone who may happen to fly an airplane. Tort law holds product manufacturers to industry standards. The knowledge of learned intermediaries and sophisticated users can cut off a manufacturer's liability for a defective product. Tort law even excuses the ignorance of those who only incidentally sell a defective product. The Restatement (Second) of Torts §289(a) admonishes that we must exercise "such attention, perception of the circumstances, memory, knowledge of other pertinent matters, intelligence, and judgment as a reasonable man would have," while §289(b) holds that we must exercise specialized knowledge or skills where we have them. Jurors are to consider how foreseeable are the untoward consequences of the allegedly negligent conduct, as in the Restatement (Second) of Torts §388 where liability exists only if the defendant "knows or has reason to know that the chattel is dangerous." Knowledge is critical in fashioning tort law rules because perception is care's attribute.

To care though, knowledge and intention are not enough because, as the saying goes, good intentions pave the road to hell. Care requires that we intend things that we can in fact accomplish. Care thus includes effectiveness or efficacy. Care without effect is merely sentimentality or (worse) hypocrisy. The distinction is like that between sympathy and compassion, the former ineffective while the latter bringing needed remedy. Care produces action of the sort that makes a difference. The parent who tells the child that the parent loves the child but fails to feed and clothe the child is not a caring parent. Actions, not words, express care. One must combine effective means with will, knowledge, and intent to avoid harm.

Tort rules and doctrines consider effectiveness or efficacy. Tort law does not require the impossible from us. Tort law judges an actor's conduct assuming the actor's physical strength, height, weight, agility, speed, and other characteristics, holding a short man only to conduct that a short man can accomplish. The Restatement (Second) of Torts §402A, comment k, excuses injury due to unavoidably unsafe (but for other reasons warranted) medical drugs and devices, while case law excuses liability for products judged defective only by later art that did not exist at the time of manufacture. Tort law would never require a lay person to perform brain surgery to save a life but certainly requires brain surgery within the standard of care when performed by trained surgeon. Care requires that one who holds oneself out as a specialist possess and exercise the skill, knowledge, and training of a specialist, even if the skill, knowledge, and training is thoroughly absent. Actor does not satisfy the standard of care by false claim that the actor is or wishes to be a healer. Appreciating risks and desiring to avoid them means nothing without the ability to accomplish the desired end. Efficacy is necessary care attribute.

Care also requires humility that we must judge others as equals even when some would wish to judge others as beneath them. Care requires those with power and means to give due regard to the wellbeing of others who have no means and power. Care does not prefer rich and powerful over poor and powerless. Care presumes that all those who exist have equal value, care itself being the intrinsic value. Accordingly, tort law holds us to higher duties to young and elderly. Tort law protects the unconscious during surgery, the seaman who falls overboard by his own neglect, and the unborn child. Tort law's eggshell-skull rule protects those who have hidden susceptibility to harm, the Restatement (Second) of Torts §435(1) stating that "the fact that the actor neither foresaw nor should have foreseen the extent of the harm or the manner in which it occurred does not prevent him from being liable." Defamation's incremental-harm doctrine protects the reputation of those who have none, while its significant-minority rule protects the reputation of those who have a reputation only among those without one. Care is humble.

Care also includes mercy or leniency, not in every case requiring full compensation for satisfaction of judgment. The extent to which the wrong requires compensation depends on the circumstances, actions, attitudes, and wellbeing of both wronged and wrongdoer. Care seldom permits punishment and retribution, while not always even requiring swift compensation. Care includes mercy because care regards both wronged and wrongdoer. The goodwill that care requires includes goodwill even to wrongdoer. Only about one in ten persons injured by another make any resort to the tort system. Nine out of ten do not, suggesting substantial mercy. Tort law applies only by the private action of private party, having no compulsion until a claimant decides to pursue relief. Even when that small fraction of possible claims results in action, about 19 out of 20 tort cases settle voluntarily before trial, again, speaking volumes about mercy, especially in that settlements tend to under-compensate the injured. Plaintiffs also prevail in not even half of jury-tried tort cases, suggesting yet more wrongdoer mercy.

Moreover, tort system depends on compensation not out of the wrongdoer's pocket but by liability insurance. Claimants seldom pursue the uninsured, while usually voluntarily limiting recovery to insurance policy limits, so that wrongdoers typically pay nothing. Tort law itself sometimes imposes a duty only when insurance will pay for the harm, for instance in suits involving intra-family or charitable immunity. Permitting liability insurer to stand for the wrong of insured is merciful contrasted to criminal or regulatory systems punishing wrongdoers. Tort law also redeems wrongdoers to good standing not only with injured but also with community, by releasing wrongdoer on payment of judgment or negotiated settlement. That redemption is so complete that it allows no recourse against the wrongdoer even should the injured person die after the release. Care's mercy and leniency are present throughout tort law.

Care balances mercy with judgment and justice. While judgment might not be our first thought about care, care is nonetheless robust enough to include judgment, robust because care requires constant action on behalf of those needing protection. *Judgment* or *justice* describes that restorative action that care requires on careless injury. Care's justice is not retributive, having nothing to do with gratifying vengeful desire to see penalty exacted. Care's justice is instead rational response to wrong, disposition to treat according to merited conduct. Justice has both public and private attributes, preserving individual peace while aggregating quickly into public order. Justice's compensatory remedy extends mercy, pardoning wrongdoer. Tort law depends on judgment and satisfaction of judgment. Tort doctrine restricts judgment to a claimant's single satisfaction. Claimants have no double dipping. Tort law grants further recourse to claimants whose loss wrongdoers only partially satisfy. Tort doctrines for contribution, comparative negligence, allocation of fault, and apportionment of damages balance judgment. Although voluntary settlement avoids formal judgment, judgment's availability provides the incentive to settle. Care does not require judgment in every case, but whether claimants choose to sue, the potential for judgment lends meaning to the entire tort system.

Care also has the character of truth, meaning the reality of circumstances and affairs. Care's truth requires that we recognize the equal interests of others. As one knows the fact and value of one's own existence, one must equally grant consciousness and value to others. Our true state of affairs is that we share existence. Confronting us with the truth of others, care requires and disposes us to give others due consideration. Tort law reflects care's truth both at its roots and doctrinal expression. Tort law conceives its duty of care as rule of reason, defined not by what any one actor subjectively believes in internal speculation but rather by objective determination based on external considerations. Tort law enforces the most-fundamental of truth between private actors that they have equal claim to existence. Tort law thus creates liability for false imprisonment and for injury caused by false words. It recognizes causes of action for false advertising, false light invasion of privacy, and fraudulent misrepresentation. It requires informed rather than uninformed consent to medical treatment. Whenever individuals speak, write, and represent to one another material to their health, reputation, and finances, tort law remedies harm that may flow from untruths manipulating circumstances and transactions.

Tort law's care is also compassionate, promoting actions to avoid and relieve harm. One can be sympathetic or pitying while at the same time causing the harm that evinces it. Villains probably often do pity their victims and may even feel some measure of sympathy. Yet one cannot be compassionate while causing unnecessary harm or unnecessarily allowing it to continue. Care involves that compassionately watchful regard for wellbeing of others. Tort law reflects compassion in its preventive and deterrent roles reducing injury, encouraging improvements in the safety of vehicles, highways, products, and medical services. Tort law then provides make-whole remedy to those harmed by carelessness. Tort law shows compassion again when measuring damages to compensate rather than punish. If tort law were merely sympathetic, it would declare injury without providing compensation. If it were retributive, it would punish wrongdoer. Instead, it compensates for harm, placing the injured in as close a position as possible to the pre-injury status or condition with recovery for medical expense, wage loss, pain and suffering, mental and emotional distress, loss of enjoyment of life, and loss of household services. Tort doctrines on collateral sources, aggravation of pre-existing conditions, and subsequent injury all reflect just that degree of assistance proportional and fitting to the injury. Compassion supports tort law.

Tort law's care is also impartial, doing for each just as circumstances rather than name, class, or reputation warrant. Care does not favor one class over another. It matters not if those for whom one should care happen to be friends or enemies, leaders or followers, native or alien. The ability to care, rather than recipient identity, determines. Care protects the weak without favoring them in administering justice. Everyone gets their due because care has equity, objectivity, fairness, proportionality, and impartiality as attributes. Tort law reflects care's impartiality. Comparative-negligence doctrine reduces the injured person's recovery by the injured person's own lack of care for the injury. Contribution rules allocate fault and apportion damages fairly among wrongdoers even where deep pockets attract claimants. Where tort law's vicarious liability holds an innocent person liable by relationship to the wrongdoer, tort law permits the innocent to shift the loss to that active wrongdoer. While tort law recognizes immunities such as for legislators and judges, it does so for public benefit rather than person interests. Tort law's care remains impartial.

Care also includes self-control. Care discourages self-seeking actions that harm interests of others. Care certainly authorizes rational choice to provide for oneself. Care does not require self-denial for its own sake. Rather, care requires setting aside selfish interests unduly conflicting with equal and greater interests of others. Preferring self over others is rational when greater good would be its results but with caution that our subjectivity makes judging it hazardous. Taking care does not leave one penniless. To the contrary, care earns good reputation. The value of action to the good of all (rather than the good only of oneself) is the only basis for preferring that action. Tort law recognizes self-control. Fiduciary duties prohibit self-seeking and self-interested transactions managing assets belonging to others. Prudent management is unselfish action promoting interests of others. Conceiving of tort law as dependent on an objective standard of conduct rests on unselfishness. Defense counsel will use evidence of actions defendant took against the defendant's own financial interest to prove defendant's care. Unselfishness is fundamental and commonly understood attribute of care.

Yet liberty is also a care attribute for tort law. Liberty in its useful sense is freedom from despotic or arbitrary authority. No law is constitutional without rational basis. Yet liberty itself depends on order and thus on reasonable self-restraint. Society without law, resting instead on the anarchic force and violence of the powerful, is not a society in which individuals have liberty. Liberty depends on reasonable authority and widespread obedience to it. Only then do individuals have meaningful opportunity to choose. Liberty arises only with that free choice. Care thus enables liberty because liberty exists only within care's generous confines. Once chosen, care then ensures liberty. Tort law ensures liberty because tort law is solely remedial, authorizing damages action rather than regulatory restriction. Tort law imposes no injunction, no prior restraint. Wrongdoers remain free not only to choose wrongs but to continue in them, even after an injury, as long as recognizing that tort law will hold them liable for that injury. Manufacturers may continue to sell a product after claims prove its defectiveness. Product recall is no part of traditional tort law. Statutes of limitation and repose grant liberty from claims after delay. Tort law grants claimants liberty to encounter open and obvious hazards, and voluntarily assume known risks. Tort law's standard of care is a law of liberty.

What, then, are carelessness's attributes? Surprisingly, care and carelessness share some attributes. Liberty is one of those shared attributes. Carelessness presumes that the actor has liberty to commit careless act. One cannot condemn as careless an actor under compulsion. Fault depends on the errant exercise of liberty. An actor may exercise liberty to accomplish cruel ends, indifferent toward cruel ends, carelessly as to whether injury results, or with reasonable care toward others. Liberty is neutral attribute, telling us nothing of the quality of the act. Yet to judge an actor careless, the actor must have liberty to act. The Restatement (Third) of Torts: Products Liability §2(b), requires for products liability that "the foreseeable risks of the product could have been reduced or

116

avoided by the adoption of a reasonable alternative design." The same is true for motor-vehicle accident, that claimant must prove that respondent could and should have taken other action. Tort doctrine on unavoidable harm, whether in sudden emergency, as to unavoidably unsafe products, or as to state-of-the-art design, all recognize that carelessness depends on liberty of putative wrongdoer to act. Carelessness's liberty appears most starkly at its furthest limits, where tort law offers remedy for horrible harms committed by demonic mass murderers and sexual deviants, for example. When actors exercise liberty for prurient and frivolous pleasures, tort law holds them liable.

Carelessness also requires will or volition, just as volition is an attribute of care. Bad desire alone is not carelessness. Tort law does not condemn harmful or reckless thoughts. Carelessness involves committing the will to pursue those thoughts. Intent is a necessary attribute of carelessness, not necessarily intent to commit harm but intent to commit the careless act. An actor cannot be careless without capability to choose care. Tort law reflects the volitional nature of carelessness by considering the actor's state of mind. Intentional torts like trespass, assault and battery, false arrest and imprisonment, conversion, and intentional infliction of emotional distress depend on the actor's willing state of mind. To commit an intentional tort, the actor must either desire harm or know of its substantial certainty. Yet torts of negligence also require volition. An actor has no liability for harmful results from an unexpected involuntary reaction. Willingness is primary attribute of carelessness.

Carelessness also includes perception or intelligence not to conform one's conduct to what reason dictates. The careless actor recognizes others whose interests could be affected by that action which the actor then contemplates – and that the actor chooses the unreasonably perilous course notwithstanding that intelligence or perception. Carelessness does not exist without known or knowable person or interest at risk. One engaging in wild acts that would be careless if placing another at risk may be perfectly careful with no one at risk. Yet where the actor knows or should know that an act places another at risk, then that perception or intelligence creates context for carelessness. Tort law recognizes

117

perception or intelligence as attribute of carelessness. Knowledge or foreseeability of potential injury is necessary in every case. Tort law's doctrine of transferred intent is an example, that it is enough that the wrongdoer intended harmful or offensive contact even when an unknown person suffers the actual wrong. Once the actor accepts untoward risk, carelessness exists whether harm befalls one or another. Tort law condemns intelligent encountering of undue risk.

Effectiveness or efficacy is also an attribute of carelessness. The actor must accomplish the unreasonable end. Acts that have no efficacy or effect in bringing about the harm are simply not the kind of carelessness that tort law condemns. Careless thoughts or even attempts to do something that would be careless if accomplished do not give rise to liability because they cause no injury. Carelessness requires effective action, even if the action is that which brings about harm. Tort law requires efficacy of carelessness by limiting liability to those instances where real and substantial harm results. Tort law does not hold propositioning an unwilling person woman to be an actionable sexual assault or ordinarily hold offensive profanity and vulgarity to be a tort. The action must be effective in causing harmful or offensive result. The impact rule still retained in some jurisdictions, and physical-manifestation-of-injury requirement in other jurisdictions, express the efficacy that tort doctrine requires as attribute of carelessness. Efficacy defines the limits of liability. Claimants must prove that the actor's conduct in fact caused the harmful result. Tort law does not condemn the idle thought but its poisonous fruit.

Although care and carelessness share attributes, carelessness has its own unique attributes. Carelessness often includes indulgence or intemperance, the opposite of care's self-control. To indulge is to pursue satisfaction beyond the need. Intemperance disregards natural and orderly bounds to appetite. Appetite has nothing wrong with it. Propensities serve important purposes. Yet when we serve the propensity rather than its purpose, appropriate pleasure becomes endangering indulgence, whether as to intoxicating drink, exciting speed, sexual satisfactions, earning profits, accumulating property, exercise of authority, or any other act. Indulgence need not be obviously corrupting in order to constitute carelessness. One can be just as intemperate as to one's own children, reputation, rest, or work. Not every careless act has indulgence or intemperance as an attribute, but many do. Tort law practitioners recognize intemperate flaws. Drunken and reckless drivers keep tort lawyers employed, as do manufacturers and retailers whom profits motivate to design and sell cheap unsafe products, home sellers who fraudulently conceal home defects, and business sellers who fraudulently inflate business values. Tort law recognizes avarice not only for liability but for punitive-damage award. Indulgence is often an attribute of carelessness.

Carelessness also has an aspect of irrationality about it. Reason perceives circumstances as they are. Rational mind comprehends circumstances and prevails with the will. With care, the will conforms conduct to reason's dictates. With carelessness, rational mind and reason do not prevail. The will instead pursues something other than what reason and rationality project. The actor chooses actions inconsistent with what reason indicates fits the circumstance. To be careless is to be unreasoning, the actor making decision or judgment that does not fit circumstances. Impulses and appetites prevail despite reason knowing better. Reason exists to speak truth to the will that the will may pursue fitting course. Carelessness arises when the will pursues course contrary to reason. We readily understand careless acts as contrary to reason in that the actor knew or should have known that continued action along that careless course would lead to harmful consequences. Careless action is irrational, stupid, unwise, and nonsensical. Tort law everywhere recognizes carelessness's unreasoning attribute. Unreasonableness is the liability standard no less in ordinary negligence cases than in products liability, premises liability, and breach of fiduciary duty. Professional malpractice provides somewhat different form of rationality standard measured by breach of the custom or standard of practice. Tort law sees irrationality as core attribute of carelessness.

Carelessness also has an aspect of selfishness about it. Interest alone is not bad or wrong. Selfishness, though, rejects fitting course of action because it does not promote some benefit to the self. Selfishness makes an end of benefiting the self, when self-benefit should remain only means to satisfy reasonable need. Selfishness makes a vice of the virtue of reasonably satisfying ordinary needs. Tort law recognizes self-interested action as an attribute of carelessness. Tort law's fiduciary duty exposes the self-interested trustee to liability in the event of fiduciary loss. The fault standard at the heart of negligence law, being objective standard, rejects subjectively selfish actions harmful to others. Professionals, for instance, must follow professional customs, not their own personal standard. To make tort law's standard subjective to the needs, qualifications, and interests of the party whose conduct causes harm would wrongly equate selfishness with reasonable care. Carelessness means that the defendant has not conformed conduct to community standard. Jurors perceive and condemn acts showing self-interest at the expense of others. Selfishness is a fundamental and commonly understood attribute of carelessness.

Partiality, prejudice, and preference can also be aspects of carelessness. Carelessness arises when an actor prefers personal interest or the interest of one over others. Preferring one interest over another can mark carelessness. Carelessness exhibits partiality to one person (whether the actor or another) over others, or to one interest over others. Preference denies the value and merit of others. Excess highway speed prefers driver and occupant interests over the safety of others. Ambulance drivers and police officers routinely speed but only out of public duty rather than personal preference. In high-speed chase with police and suspect vehicles moving at same rate of speed, we judge only the latter careless because of the suspect's preferring own freedom over safety of those along the highway. Tort law recognizes partiality as an attribute of carelessness. Carelessness has its root in disregarding the wellbeing of others but its full flower in partiality's active opposition to those others.

Carelessness indeed often reflects direct opposition to good, as many tort rules and doctrines recognize. Intentional torts create liability for assault and battery, false imprisonment, trespass, and other wrongs where the intent is to harm. Tort law creates liability for the intentional infliction of severe emotional distress, by outrageous acts. Tort law distinguishes intentional from merely negligent torts for purposes of awarding punitive damages, which tort law also authorizes for recklessness, willfulness, or wantonness toward the victim's safety. Cruelty, or perverse satisfaction in loss or harm of another, can be an aspect of carelessness. The careless often know whom their negligent acts affect but reflect hard hearts toward them, sometimes even speaking poorly of them. Tort law may eliminate parental immunity and hold parents liable for their child's particularly cruel wrong. Cruel intent may also overcome governmental immunity. Cruelty in marriage can establish grounds for tort action within divorce in rare cases. Constitutional tort actions arise for cruel and unusual punishment. Tort law opposes cruelty as an attribute of carelessness.

Carelessness also includes an attribute of disproportionality. Order in society requires that one respect the interests of one's neighbor as much as one's own interests. Carelessness lacks that proportion, skewing interests and other considerations. When the tort claimant can show that the defendant gave disproportionate regard to anything over the claimant's safety interests, the claimant will have established liability. For example, the Restatement (Second) of Torts §293 uses risk-magnitude analysis to determine reasonable care, weighing the social value of imperiled interests. The Restatement (Second) of Torts §519(1) grants strict liability for harm caused by abnormally dangerous activities when their dangers are greater than the value they contribute. The Restatement (Second) of Torts §402A tests liability for defective products by determining whether the defendant balanced regard for the safety of those who may be injured by its product. Products liability depends on balancing risk against utility. Tort law finds carelessness when risk is disproportionate to utility. Carelessness implies lack of balance and proportion.

Falsehood, inaccuracy, or error is likewise an aspect of carelessness. Tort law condemns not only direct falsehoods like misrepresentation and defamation but also indirect and implied falsehoods like breach of warranty and conversion. Tort law further imposes negligence liability when an actor falsely presumes to afford the actor or others greater regard than that for the injured victim. Carelessness falsely distorts the true state of relationship and circumstances in favor of risking others unduly. Tort law permits no individual to stand above and apart from the duty of care except in doctrines of immunity that preserve and promote truths about the immune person's status. Tort law eliminates immunity when the individual exceeds the scope of the authority or role that warranted the immunity. Tort law condemns false assertions of role, authority, and value, holding liable not only the knowing liar but also the careless exaggerator and distorter.

These then are attributes of care and carelessness, reflected in tort cases, rules, and doctrines. Law roots civil liability in these attributes, in care's rich soil. Tort law finds its heart, core, comprehensiveness, grandeur, elegance, balance, nuance, subtlety, and source in promoting wellbeing through care toward one another. We should know, respect, preserve, and celebrate care's basis for tort law to design and balance the tort system properly, not for special interests of perpetrators or victims but for the value of all constituencies in all their capacities and interests. The particular tort system's form may not ultimately matter as long as we preserve care as its fundamental goal and value. Tort systems do not have to look like ours, and ours may need modification. Yet we must know its end in care, as universal value of individual good. Care and carelessness share and diverge in attributes, those attributes so deeply informing life in society as to justify and inform law itself.

Chapter 8

Discarding the Past

Law scholars dispute tort law's origins in care and in doing so discard its profound past. Justice Oliver Wendell Holmes wrote in his famous 1881 book *The Common Law* that primitive tort law began with intentional of wrongs generating moral outrage and revenge but gradually developed toward an external negligence and then strict-liability standard. In 1894, celebrated law scholar John Henry Wigmore asserted the opposite view in an article *Responsibility for Tortious Acts* published in the Harvard Law Review. Wigmore held that primitive tort law began with strict liability, making no distinction as to moral culpability and intent, but gradually developed toward moral intentional tort and negligence standards. Wigmore assumed that an "essentially superstitious and irrational spirit [] pervaded the jural doings of primitive society," without identifying which primitive societies. In 1908, another scholar James Barr Ames asserted a similar view in an article *Law and Morals* published in the Harvard Law Review that "early law is formal and unmoral" compared to modern law.

Despite that they had tort law developing in opposite directions, both Holmes and Wigmore presumed that tort law was developing resolutely upward over the ages. They both believed that tort law was improving even though in opposite directions. They also both placed tort law's roots in medieval England after the 1066 A.D. Norman conquest. The Holmes and Wigmore views that a previously absent or at best barbarous tort law emerged from medieval England remains the dominant view among law scholars and commentators. Law review articles written by leading tort law scholars and published in respected journals, like Malone's *Ruminations on the Role of Fault in the History of the Common Law of Torts*, hold to the view that tort law in general and fault-based tort law in particular are recent evolutions. The leading tort law student casebooks, including the venerable Prosser torts casebook in its eleventh edition, teach substantially the same view in American law schools.

Prior chapters of this book have shown that the view that a previously absent or at best primitive tort law arose from medieval England is an interesting but largely false assertion. Scholars have been wrong before. What is unusual though is that these views on the relatively recent origin of fault-based tort law, rather than its demonstrated antiquity, have persisted despite shown wrong. Not long after Holmes, Wigmore, and Ames published their erroneous views, in 1918 Nathan Isaacs published (also in the Harvard Law Review) that they were wrong, showing instead that tort law rules of ordinary care existed right back through pre-Norman sources like the 1027 A.D. Winchester Code of King Cnut, the 901 A.D. code of King Alfred, the circa 600 A.D. Germanic Laws of King Ethelbert, all the way back to the ancient mosaic law of the Torah. Isaacs concluded in the 1918 Harvard Law Review that

> [i]f . . . we stop at the dawn of English legal history we find the fault basis clearly assumed. Indeed if we read the medieval dooms through, instead of stopping at curious phrases, we shall find that the most striking principle that runs through them is a rough adjustment of liability to fault.

Isaacs deduced that "the history of tort law records lapses from the moral fault basis and returns to it, rather than a single movement in any one direction," that which he also called "swings of a pendulum...." Another tort law scholar Thomas Beven, writing in 1895 just before the ascendancy of Holmes and Wigmore, knew the ancient Roman tort laws too well to accept Holmes' and Wigmore's surprising assumption that tort law had originated in and developed from medieval England. Indeed Beven believed that English and American tort law drew directly, or at least could well have drawn, on the ancient Roman negligence laws.

Since the early part of the 20th century, other scholars have traced intentional torts, negligence, strict liability, fixed and variable compensation, and indirect causation back through history to the even earlier pre-mosaic sources. In 1966 Reuven Yaron wrote of the tort rules in Near Eastern laws predating the biblical Book of the Covenant, in *The Goring Ox in Near Eastern Laws*. In 1975 Bernard Jackson published his comparative legal history studies on Jewish antiquity, followed later by his work on models of development in ancient legal history, both showing the existence and sensitivity in the ancient texts of tort law rules of all kinds. In 1981, the American Philosophical Society published posthumously J.J. Finkelstein's draft summary of his long-running research on ancient Mesopotamian legal texts, *The Ox that Gored*, in which Finkelstein used the ancient texts' cultural contexts to demonstrate their remarkable sensitivity to tort liability. In 1986, Saul Levmore wrote of the ancient codes' "remarkable degree of variety" and their "uniform deterrence" of negligent acts, in *Rethinking Comparative Law: Variety and Uniformity in Ancient and Modern Tort Law*. In 1999, Anne Fitzpatrick-McKinley showed the coherent conceptual system behind the ancient texts and their liability systems, in *The Transformation of Torah from Scribal Advice to Law*. The sum of these works shows that a meaningfully sensitive tort law has been around for at least 2,500 years longer than Holmes, Wigmore, and other recent commentators give it credit.

Why then the persistence of the traditional view that tort law is recent evolution? Perhaps it is as Isaacs wrote that we find it "difficult to escape the tyranny of popular ideas!" Or maybe as Isaacs also ventured the Darwinian view of tort law's evolution seems so "esoteric and learned." The challenge of understanding ancient texts opens a door to confusion over those sources. Or it may be as Jackson surmised, that because ancient laws "encompassed far more than their modern counterparts" that their study within contemporary disciplinary boundaries "produces only historical distortion." We may have psychological desire that our laws demonstrate what we earnestly wish to believe, that we are better than our ancestors. Daube concludes that the view that direct causation in the ancient texts shows a primitive incapacity is "founded on a naïve belief (which captured the world of anthropology, ancient history and classics in the 19th century) in a progress of mankind from childishness to intelligence." That the rigidity of some ancient laws is due to childish inability to grasp less-obvious concepts is baseless. "Nothing," concludes Daube, "could be further from the truth" reflected by close and fair study of the ancient texts. Such interpretations are "due to an underrating of the intellectual powers of people in that age."

Yet to know why erroneous views of tort law history persist requires first knowing more about how those erroneous views arose. When Holmes first set forth in *The Common Law* the popular but false view of tort law's development, he was somewhat less colorful than others have been in describing the assumedly barbaric cultures from whence tort law purportedly issued but no less sure of his Darwinian footing. To Holmes, the early law writers could, in pre-developed vengeful state, discern only the simplest and most pronounced of tort cases. "Vengeance imports a feeling of blame and an opinion, however distorted by passion, that a wrong has been done," Holmes wrote, leading him to perhaps his most famous tort law quip that "even a dog distinguishes between being stumbled over and being kicked." Holmes was also quick to associate the purportedly primitive laws of these barbaric cultures with religion, their having "naturally adopted the vocabulary, and in some degree the tests of morals." Holmes in the same breath gave tort law its evolutionary direction toward negligence, that "as the law has grown even when its standards have continued to model themselves upon those of morality, they have necessarily become external" standards measured against whether the wrongdoer's "conduct would have been wrong in the fair average member of the community, whom he is expected to equal at his peril."

Holmes briefly considered that his "order of development is not quite consistent" with the contrary (though still Darwinian) view held by Wigmore and others "that it was a characteristic of early law not to penetrate beyond the external visible fact" of the occurrence and injury. But Holmes promptly rejected that "whatever may have been the early law," his account "shows the starting point" based on "actual intent and actual personal culpability." Tort law's "transformation" from vengeance to independent standards showed that "the law has grown, without a break, from barbarism to civilization." "Learned men," Holmes wrote in perhaps his most paternalistic statement, "have been ready to find a reason in the personification of inanimate nature common to savages and children, and there is much to confirm this view." To Holmes, man had not until recently sufficiently developed his social conventions to bring forth the flower of tort law. The ancients were primitive savages, like children.

Though he held to the opposite direction of tort law's development, Wigmore was equally or even more committed to his same view that tort law was evolutionary. "Primitive" law "raised no issue as to the presence or absence of a design or intent," held Wigmore, directly contrary to Holmes' starting point that actual intent and personal culpability were liability's historical starting point. Indeed to Wigmore, "it did not even distinguish in its earlier phases between accidental and intentional injuries," again directly contrary to Holmes who had intent (vengeance) as the starting point. Rather, to Wigmore, "the indiscriminate liability of primitive times stands for an instinctive impulse, guided by superstition, to visit with vengeance, the visible source, whatever it be—human or animal, witting or unwitting—of the evil result." To Wigmore, the primitive mind was incapable of moral distinctions. In so stating, Wigmore (like Holmes) linked "primitive" law with religious, magical, animistic, and other supernatural influences, attributing law's undeveloped state to "the essentially superstitious and irrational spirit which pervaded the jural doings of primitive society." Wigmore supported his premise as to the primitive nature of pre-Norman English law, by using its presumed judgment upon animals as well as humans. To Wigmore, the primitive mind was incapable of distinguishing between the capability of humans and incapability of animals to make and follow moral judgments.

The majority of influential early commentators agreed with Wigmore rather than Holmes on the pattern of development but shared the view of both Holmes and Wigmore that tort law existed only in primitive form before this mixed-bag development took place.   In 1905, Professor Bohlen, who reported the Restatement (First) of Torts and whom some recognize as the father of modern tort law, traced the basis for tort law obligations to that same historical period of the English writs of trespass and case, in his well-known article *The Basis of Affirmative Obligations in the Law of Tort*.   In 1906, Street aimed to discover "the true path of legal evolution" in his extensive summary of tort law *The Foundations of Legal Liability: Vol. I, Theory and Principles of Tort*. Though Street's preface mentioned Holmes, Street's summary of the historical development of tort law was that of Wigmore to whom Street gave specific credit.   Strict liability for immediate consequences, whether intentional, negligent, or accidental without fault, "seems to be fundamentally inherent in the primary stages of legal thought," Street summarized.   Street drew that for "many hundred years" "the conception of negligence" was "unknown to the law of trespass" the basis for which was instead strict liability.   "[T]he common law was very slow in giving full recognition" to the essential role played by negligence because "an arbitrary presumption seems to suppress the idea of negligence entirely."   Thus Wigmore's view took hold: jurists of late-medieval England wrote fundamental principles of tort law on strict liability's blank slate, a slate left blank because its "primitive" guardians knew little of how to think and write about care for one another as tort law's organizing principle.

The great thinkers of Wigmore's day mostly agreed.   In 1908, Ames also agreed with Wigmore that "early law is formal and unmoral" but that "[t]he ethical standard of reasonable conduct has replaced the unmoral standard of acting at one's peril."   "The early law," Ames explained in reference to the earliest extant English cases, "asked simply, 'Did the defendant do the physical act which damaged the plaintiff?'"   "The law of today," Ames continued, "asks the further question, 'Was the act blameworthy?'"   "[T]he spirit of reform" has "during the last six hundred years [] been bringing our system of law more and more into harmony with moral principles," Ames concluded.

Writing in the same generation in the second volume of *History of English Law*, Pollock agreed with Ames and Wigmore that "'[i]n a rude state of society the desire of vengeance is measured by the harm actually suffered and not by any consideration of the actor's intention,'" whereas in comparison the law then extant depended on a showing of carelessness or unlawful intention. Pollock concluded that "'hence the archaic law of injuries is a law of absolute liability for the direct consequences of a man's acts tempered only by partial exceptions in the hardest cases.'" Others, including Whittier and Ballantine both published in the Harvard Law Review, agreed not only with Wigmore as to the origins of tort law in absolute liability but also (through a bit of reformist history) mistakenly lumping Holmes in with Wigmore on that view. They recruited a posthumous Holmes to the Wigmore view Holmes had rejected while alive. Wigmore's influence on the origin of tort law became so pronounced that in 1926 Winfield proclaimed in *The History of Negligence in the Law of Torts* that his own similar history had only "with a certain amount of qualification and addition, made good the predictions of a brilliant American writer [Wigmore] as to its probable course."

One finds no difficulty tracing the more-general source of these tort law views. These scholars all drew from the same well as Main in his 1886 *Dissertations on Early Law and Custom* and in his 1906 *Ancient Law: Its Connection with the Early History of Society and Its Relation to Modern Ideas*, as well as on Lea's *Superstition and Force*. In these works, Main and Lea stated the definitive Darwinist view of law as having originated in the medieval blood feud. Darwin's theories of the origin of species also created a legal school. Main popularized law's Darwinian view, writing of communities in their "infancy" and "primitive seats" the "upward march" of which "is almost certain." Main held that the ancients had only a primitive mental capacity incapable of differentiating important concepts. To support his thesis, Main surmised that law grew out of a naïve mix of morals and religion, where the ancients "mingled up religious, civil, and merely moral ordinances, without any regard to essential differences in their character," that being "consistent with all we know of early thought" before the "severance of law from morality, and of religion from law" in "the later stages of mental progress." "There is no system of recorded law, literally from China to Peru,"

Main concluded, "which, when it first emerges into notice, is not seen to be entangled with religious ritual and observance."

Jackson indicates that although evidence discredited the Darwinist view of legal development, its suppressed influence remains. The writing of Main "implanted in the contemporary legal mind the view that early cultures [we]re incapable of discriminating between religious and legal obligation." We are now in a period in which scholars use data with little concern for theory. The traditional Wigmore view thus remains shibboleth among contemporary law commentators, even if they no longer embrace Wigmore's extraordinarily naïve social Darwinism. Today's pragmatic materialism does little to correct Darwinist distortions. For example, in classic Darwinist summary of the Wigmore view, Malone wrote in 1970 that negligence law "is not likely to come into being until society has reached a stage where diverse economic and social needs have emerged and are in lively competition with each other." To Malone, negligence law arose as fittest mutant among relatively recent competition of laws and interests. Malone reiterated the accepted view that "[t]he primordial seed from which both crime and tort were to generate was the blood feud that was characteristic of any barbaric society organized along the lines of blood kinship" consistent with "the wholly amoral character of early law." Only then did "tort liability gradually emerge[] from its medieval chrysalis."

Rabin in his 1981 *The Historical Development of the Fault Principle: A Reinterpretation* held similarly that negligence law was the 19th century's progressive reaction to industrialization in the face of pre-existing no-liability or strict-liability law regimes. He thus took the view of Winfield so many years before him. Similarly, Silver would write in 1992 in his 100-year summary of medical malpractice laws that the roots of negligence are in 14th-century common law. Feldman agreed in 2000 that "the substantive law of negligence emerged from the old common law forms of action, particularly trespass and trespass on the case," which did not consider intent or carelessness to be an element. Among current commentators, the Wigmore view remains the staple. As Jackson lamented, "A combination of nineteenth century evolutionism and twentieth century pragmatism produces an attitude which views the ancient texts as manifestations of primitive or archaic minds, and therefore of no contemporary interest."

Commentators were repeating and reinforcing what they would have learned from the popular law school casebooks, which continue to teach that tort law in general and fault-based tort law in particular are modern developments arising out of an early English common law. The most-popular law student torts casebook, Prosser, continues to inculcate that the "more generally accepted theory" is Wigmore's that tort law "began by imposing liability on those who caused physical harm, and gradually developed toward the acceptance of moral standards as the basis of liability." The Prosser casebook opens under the first chapter title "Development of Liability Based Upon Fault" and then recites in Wigmore vein that "[c]ertainly at one time the law was not very much concerned with the moral responsibility of the defendant." Prosser then traces tort law's "historical origins" through medieval and later English cases citing as commentary not only Wigmore and Ames (as well as giving brief mention to Holmes) but also Woodbine and Maitland. Prosser even offers the 1850 Massachusetts case Brown v Kendall with the explanation that "[t]his decision is the earliest clear statement of the rule commonly applied: liability must be based on legal fault." Prosser then introduces negligence as subject with the statement that it "was scarcely recognized as a separate tort before the earlier part of the nineteenth century" and cites only Wigmore and his student Winfield "[f]or the history of negligence in early law, and its development as an independent tort...."

Vetri's casebook seconds Prosser that "[i]n the beginning, crime and tort were much the same in scope" but that tort law developed in an "evolutionary period" out of the king's courts. Vetri attributes the only "difference of view among legal scholars about the development of negligence law" to whether that development was to assist rising industrial interests or recognize rising morality. Granted, Prosser briefly cites Isaacs. And Vetri makes a curious reference to the "ancient usage of the word 'trespass'" "in the modern day version of the Lord's Prayer." But neither Prosser nor Vetri suggest what the historical record shows that fault-based liability and other important features of tort law existed in many ancient codes long before their appearance in the laws of medieval England or indeed that the common law explicitly drew on those ancient sources in adapting them to medieval and modern cultures. Other casebooks and hornbooks uniformly follow suit.

Strange the Wigmore view should have seemed to the modern materialist mind, that morality would emerge from immorality, and that negligence would emerge from strict liability (or its opposite that strict liability would emerge from negligence), in essence that something should emerge from nothing. That incongruity should have been especially obvious given what Sherman wrote in 1917 that "[t]he maxim of the philosophers Ex nihilo nihil fit—'something does not come from nothing'—may be taken as the keynote to all legal history." Indeed, those following Wigmore's ahistorical Darwinist view attributed the ancient's purportedly primitive view to their law being mixed up with magic, religion, and animism. As Kelsen wrote in 1945 in his *General Theory of Law and State*, "In primitive law, animals, and even plants and other inanimate objects are often treated in the same way as human beings and are, in particular, punished. However, this must be seen in its connection with the animism of primitive man."

Yet scholarship now shows this assumption wrong. Jackson writes that since Main's day when scholars commonly accepted that law only gradually and recently became secular in nature, new evidence has shown the opposite that law was quite secular in nature until later grounded and justified by religious reference. Fitzpatrick-McKinley writes that crisis legitimating the Israelite leadership, "brought about by the increased stratification of Israelite society," led to the grounding of a previously secular law in the will of God. "[T]he process is one of a development from secular to sacral law," not sacred to secular, Fitzpatrick-McKinley concluded. The new Israelite monarchy disrupted that ancient society's previous unity based on family clan. As Israelite society diversified, resulting disunity created not only need for law to protect those left to the margins but moreover need to ground law beyond secular common interest no longer so apparent. As chapters above show, the Laws of Eshnunna and Code of Hammurabi predating the Israelite religious covenant were largely secular in nature. History does not support the Darwinist premise that the law of liability began as mixed with magic or religion. The above chapters show that ancient tort law included variations on present-day tort liability including intentional torts, negligence, and strict liability, indirect causation, and fixed versus variable compensation.

If scholars still propounding Wigmore's view are wrong in their treatment of the ancient texts, were they any more right in their justification of their own view? By attributing negligence's immaculate conception to "spirits of reform" (Ames), "subconscious appreciation" (Winfield), and "primordial seeds" of unidentified source and origin (Malone), proponents of the Wigmore view rested their own case on improbable and indeed supernatural assertions. Reasoning of that kind, if one can call it reasoning, is stock in trade of the superstitious, whom these Darwinists, guilty of it themselves, condemned. Commentators who correct Darwinian inaccuracies also excuse their 19th-century excesses. As Isaacs wrote in apology for his predecessors, "When Oliver Wendell Holmes wrote, Bratton's Note-Book lay undiscovered; Maitland had not yet opened up to us the storehouse of thirteenth-century law; the great 'History' was undreamt of; Dr. Liebermann was just beginning to get interested in Anglo-Saxon laws and Twiss was still pouring confusion on the text of Bratton." Jackson grants that "considerable evidence has come to light of 'law-codes' from the ancient Near East" since Main's day. Although scholars published the Code of Hammurabi around 1902, scholars had not translated the Laws of Eshnunna into until 1948, long after Wigmore, Holmes, and Ames wrote. Isaacs made it clear that he did not intend to speak disrespectfully of his predecessors, "at least not here, with the grand old portrait of Timothy Walker, the author of 'American Law' and the founder of this school, staring down at me from over my desk as I write."

That tort law would lose its long-known roots beginning just in 1894 with Holmes' publication of *The Common Law* holds special irony. Just the year before in 1893, the leading law writer of the age before Holmes, Justice Thomas Cooley, warned in an article titled *The Administration of Justice in the United States of America in Civil Cases,* "Whoever would make himself familiar with the administration of justice in any country needs first of all to understand the source of its laws...." Justice Cooley was not ready to cut and ignore law's roots. Yet Holmes' doing so may not have been irony at all but rather intention. Justice Cooley spoke similar words of warning (in a rebuke that must have embarrassed and grieved the sensitive Justice Cooley) to Holmes and the other luminaries gathered for Harvard's 250th anniversary, where Cooley received an honorary law degree. Justice Cooley told the assembled elite,

> we fail to appreciate the dignity of our profession if we look for it either in profundity of learning or in forensic triumphs. . . . [I]ts reason for being must be found in the effective aid it renders to justice, and in the sense it gives of public security through its steady support of public order. These are commonplaces, but the strength of the law lies in its commonplace character; and it becomes feeble and untrustworthy when it expresses something different from the common thoughts of men.

Holmes was intent on conceiving of law as (in his own words) "a field for the lightning of genius," meaning his genius and the genius of others like him, to heed Justice Cooley's warning that law must exist humbly for the steady support of order. Holmes hoped that from law "may fly sparks that shall set free in some genius his explosive message," perhaps the message of Holmes' contemporary Nietzsche that man was to live for his own glory now that God (Nietzsche held) was dead. The Holmes view came to dominate American law. Holmes had the next laugh, even if not the last laugh. The view remains even into this generation of scholars that a nascent tort law somehow arose out of "medieval chrysalis" for brilliant American judges like Holmes to shape. See now how some of those brilliant 20th-century jurists fared casting tort law free from its ancient foundations, under Darwinian residue with the rise of modern legal realism.

Chapter 9

Losing the Foundation

When tort law lost its history, it also lost its foundation. As the previous chapter briefly notes, Professor Francis Bohlen was the reporter for the American Law Institute's Restatement (First) of Torts and thus a father to modern American tort law. Over one-hundred years ago in 1905, before undertaking drafting and reporting of the First Restatement, Professor Bohlen wrote an article *The Basis of Affirmative Obligations in the Law of Tort*. The leading torts casebook Prosser today still cites Professor Bohlen's 1905 article and indeed still pictures Professor Bohlen. So what did Professor Bohlen write over one-hundred years ago during the age of Wigmore and Holmes about the basis of tort law? Professor Bohlen wrote that it was unknown. Professor Bohlen wrote that try as they might, law scholars had not succeeded in discovering the ground or foundation of tort law:

> It is surprising to find that every attempt to announce either judicially or in text-books any inclusive affirmative principle of the origin of the duty of care, the primary fundamental requisite, has been unsuccessful.

Despite his alluring title that he would write of the justification for tort law, Professor Bohlen did not do so. Rather, his article argued that American tort law's historical antecedents were in the English common law of contract, deceit, and assumpsit. Drawing on tort law's purported medieval-England contract origins, Professor Bohlen ventured that "[a]ll affirmative duties may truly be termed assumptional and founded upon consideration," as if each should choose whether to submit and with whom to submit to tort law's duty of care, based on some benefit made in the bargain. The law bases contracts on voluntary agreement with something exchanged in the bargain, and so, Professor Bohlen argued, should tort law.

Tort law actually imposes duties on those who do not wish to accept them and does so between perfect strangers who have had no dealings whatsoever. We may wish to drive our vehicles as fast and furious as we find convenient or exhilarating, but we nonetheless owe duties of reasonable care to every stranger whom we place in peril by doing so. Professor Bohlen's assertion that tort law duties depend on voluntary assent and consideration seems quaint. Think of our highway carnage, lawsuits out of which comprise the substantial majority of tort litigation. Most torts happen between strangers who assume nothing contractual in nature toward one another and provide one another no consideration. While still stating that "[s]uch obligations arise only when assumed," Professor Bohlen elsewhere conceded that tort duties "are not the creatures wholly of consent" but "may be annexed to the performance of certain acts...."

As to the basis for "annexation" of duties, Professor Bohlen surmised that "if done the duties follow as a matter resting wholly on the policy of law, that policy which protects the rights of citizens from positive injury." Professor Bohlen offered no further basis for that presumed "policy of law" to protect citizens from injury. Unfortunately, suggesting that policy of law grounds a legal obligation is mere tautology until one articulates the policy basis. Saying that we have a tort duty not to injure because we have a policy of law to protect adds little to an inquiry for the basis of affirmative obligation. This unsatisfying conclusion is what Professor Bohlen admitted in the quote at the beginning of this chapter that he and other scholars recognized little regarding the source or foundation of tort law.

The Darwinism of Bohlen's day had hidden from view tort law's ancient secular history, roots in care, divine reflection in Jesus' Golden Rule, natural description at Renaissance dawn, Declaration as founding of American law, and necessary place as Kant's categorical imperative. Surprising, yes, as Professor Bohlen wrote a century ago, but disappointing also, because law systems must correctly and securely ground obligations that they impose, or they will reveal defects in development, reform, and practice. We often say that those who do not know their history are doomed to repeat it. The greater danger is not to know the signs and distortions of one's own times, measured against timeless justification or ground. The greater danger is to drown in the sea in which one swims than to be struck by the ship that would rescue. Law must define the basis for tort law's obligations so as not to err in its reform under the influences of popular but passing peculiarities.

The peril to losing tort law's mooring in the intrinsically valuable and socially critical attributes of care is great. The moment we regard others as less valuable than ourselves, we assume a position of substantial hazard. Not only do we then fail to bear fruit in our own lives, but the carelessness that we inevitably then exhibit harms others. The sheer quantity of modern-day interactions hurtling down freeways, performing hundreds of surgeries, or engaging in thousands of financial transactions ensures that a root of carelessness will quickly bring forth its thorns. When the law fails to recognize the value of others, society's fabric tears.

Knowing tort duty's justification benefits practitioners who advocate it, judges who apply it, and legislators who increasingly determine and alter its scope and contours. How can one claim, defend, preserve, or reform the extent of obligation without knowing its basis? The value of inquiry into tort law's justification is substantial considering tort law's phenomenal character, imposing as it does duty so pervasive as to govern all social interaction. Duty exists everywhere, at all times, in all situations, and is yet innately nuanced to fit every such situation. Never does duty impose less than that which works equity among those whom it governs. Tort law is further an entirely remedial and fully redemptive law, restoring and regenerating rather than exacting merciless penalty. Tort law none of criminal law's diminishing necessities, intent instead to restore those who require its assistance, satisfy judgment, and release those who have transgressed its gentle bounds, often (with the availability of insurance) without any substantive sanction whatever. We must regain the great law of care's source and foundation.

Several ongoing trends make especially acute the challenge to recognize tort law's justification. Reasons to know tort law's basis today include at least: (1) tort law's politicization, as liability rules become the subject of partisan political campaigns; (2) industry advertising regarding tort law, unconnected with political campaigns; (3) that legislation now dramatically reshapes tort law, once rooted in the common law; (4) public perception of tort law as beholden to special interests; and (5) new Supreme Court challenges in other fields of law to define law's justification.

The first two of these developments, tort law as common subject in political campaigns and public advertising, show the need for greater understanding as to the law's basis, in order that participants inform public debate. Increased political involvement in the judiciary is a well-recognized phenomenon. The American Bar Association's Commission on the 21st Century Judiciary titled its report *Justice in Jeopardy*. We have on the one hand political candidates crying the need to reform medical-malpractice laws to give doctors greater freedom but, on the other hand, studies showing tens of thousands killed or injured each year due to medical malpractice with tiny percentage, resulting in tort compensation. Debate between opposing views does little more than polarize when scholars offer no center ground for opposing constituencies. If politicians and the public cannot appeal to tort law's grounding, then how can the public make these important political and policy judgments?

The same is true as to industry advertising on tort-law issues. Insurance-industry billboards show insurance claimants going to jail for insurance fraud. Public appeals of this type can only skew the debate, opening the door to dramatic legislative and judicial reshaping of tort law benefitting special lobbies and interests while harming the injured and destitute, when the public knows little about tort law's underpinning care and the eleemosynary role insurance plays in providing it. Scholars should find it no accident that tort law becomes beholden to special interests when its reformers and defenders are unable to articulate adequate basis for it. How can advocate, legislator, judge, or jury draw tort law's liability line to reflect individual, professional, industry, social, and community interests without knowing the grounds for its drawing?

Another challenge to tort law to define its basis has come with the Supreme Court's renewed line of substantive-due-process cases. Though the cases have had little to do directly with tort law, they challenge scholars to define again the basis for legal obligation. The same pragmatic, subjectivist, and materialist views shaping the Court's substantive-due-process decisions are also shaping tort law, decisions that expressly reject as basis for legal obligation history, tradition, customs, codes, and precedents. The Court has held that "conceptions of right and acceptable behavior" held "for centuries" by "many persons" on the basis of "profound and deep convictions" nevertheless "do not answer the question" of "the power of the State to enforce these views on the whole society," and that traditional views of "the governing majority" as to the fitness of acts "is not a sufficient reason for upholding a law...." If history, tradition, custom, codes, and precedent do not justify law, what then does?

Scholars once accepted that law could ground duties of care in the common law like the old English strict-liability case *Rylands v Fletcher*, Justice Cardozo's proximate cause case *Palsgraf v Long Island R. Co.*, and other venerable cases supporting modern tort law's doctrines. At the dawn of tort law's modern era, judges and treatise writers accepted the common law as the basis of tort law, as the common law was in other law fields. Consider again Justice Cooley writing in 1893 on the American administration of civil justice:

> [T]he common law in what [the American people] understood to be its purity was unhesitatingly made the basis of their civil rights, and was administered in all their primitive jurisdictions. * * *
>
> It is upon this common law therefore as perpetuated in the several states, that their citizens still rely for the definition of fundamental rights, and for a general indication of the remedies to which they may resort for redress when wrongs are suffered. * * *

141

As the rules of the common law had their origin in rough and uncultured ages, they were not without features of wrong and hardship, but for the most part they were founded on principles of immutable justice, and the changes which have been made of them in America have been gradual and for the most part well considered.

Yet today, none finds it sufficient to say that tort law's duty of care comes from the common law, or indeed that we have always or traditionally offered to one another that care that the majority in civil society always feels to be due. Nor should that basis be sufficient. We should articulate more of the root or ground for this extraordinary duty, beyond that it has always existed. It neither satisfies the mind nor guides the reformer to say that we have a rule of duty because we have always had such rule. Habit is certainly a reliable guide for many things. We would be lost without it. Habits though are not enough when the conscience of the age challenges us to rethink and reshape rules defining tort law's duty of care.

Where then to ground tort law, if not in history and tradition? As we have just seen, the Supreme Court and other appellate courts challenge us to do more than ground law in the governing majority's legislative codes. One might think that codes are not so suspect a place to look for justification for the obligations the law imposes upon us. Legislatures tend to base codes on the fitness of their strictures to the nature and relation of those whom the codes authorize and restrict. A code for stevedores must have to do with loading and unloading ships. Legislation would presumably define the stevedores' code by conduct that stevedores require of one another to do what they must accomplish. Codes, whether ancient rules for social behavior or modern rules for technical craft, are generally reliable place to justify particular obligations in one setting or another. The Supreme Court is right about the limitation of grounding law in code in this sense: rules cannot find ultimate ground in rules. Rules do not exist for the sake of rules. To ground rule in rule is little more than to justify means by means rather than by end. We must ground rules in something other than rules and rather in ultimate end. Just as justifying obligation by history or tradition, by saying that we have always done it that way, is insufficient foundation, so too insufficient is justifying obligation by code, by saying rules justify rules.

In any case, codes seldom fix tort duties. Case law generally holds that criminal statutes, government regulations, industry standards, and ethical codes do not establish the full extent of care's duty, although they may evidence its scope. For example, Congress expressly provided in 29 USC §653(b)(4) that OSHA regulations neither enlarge nor diminish civil liability. Likewise, the American Bar Association's Model Rules of Professional Conduct prohibit use of rule violation to prove breach of civil duty of care. Codes are not tort law's root or basis. Where if not in history, tradition, custom, codes, or precedent is the foundation?

In rejecting these traditional grounds for law, the Supreme Court justified a new liberty interest in the "autonomy of self" "in both its spatial and more transcendent dimensions...." The Court's self-expressive and transcendent get-out-of-my-space autonomy appears contrary to tort law's care duty. To be *autonomous* means to direct one's self. Autonomous self acts free from influence or control of others, perhaps even from need to regard others. Tort law on the other hand imposes duty to constrain self in the equal interests of others, nearly the opposite of autonomy. To be entirely self-directed and self-expressive (autonomous) rules out interests of others, when tort law requires that one bend will and conform conduct to respect others' interests. Tort law addresses interaction and interdependence rather than independence.

Indeed, tort law's duty is surely so powerful as to invade and modulate constitutionally protected autonomy. While the Supreme Court has held states unable to enforce sodomy laws in private places, if one partner tortuously injured another even in a transcendent act of self-expression, tort law would surely protect and compensate the injured partner. In granting a sphere of self-expressive autonomy, the Supreme Court was certainly not authorizing sexual assault. Autonomy has its limits, imposed by no less than tort law's humble care duty. Tort law (not to mention criminal law) gives us endless cases arising out of careless and malicious sexual expression. Transcending rules in self-expressive autonomy is no grounding for tort law. Why do we even have tort law? Why do we owe one another anything at all?

Consider how American courts deciding tort law cases in the last century have struggled with this question since Holmes, Wigmore, and Bohlen. Citing Professor Bohlen's article as justification, Justice Benjamin Cardozo in the seminal 1916 case *MacPherson v Buick Motor Co.* took a major step toward creating modern products-liability law. That step was to abolish the need for a contract relationship as a requirement for product-liability negligence actions. No longer would law restrict products-liability actions to only those claimants who had purchased the injury-causing product. After *MacPherson*, anyone who the manufacturer should have foreseen that the product could injure would if injured have a products-liability action. Justice Cardozo stated what he had just done, in among the grandest and most-mystifying of statements ever written about tort law, that,

> We have put aside the notion that the duty to safeguard life and limb, when the consequences of negligence may be foreseen, grows out of contract and nothing else. We have put the source of the obligation where it ought to be. We have put its source in the law.

Like Professor Bohlen's "policy to protect," Justice Cardozo's "source in the law" statement grows more opaque the longer one looks at it. Where else but *in the law* would one expect to find law's duties? Tautologies can be grand and satisfying. Yet the more-interesting and valid inquiry is that source's ground or justification. In *MacPherson* Justice Cardozo had an opportunity to state the ground for obligations of care, without respect to bargains the parties made between them. Justice Cardozo needed that justification, as his citation to Professor Bohlen's article purporting to state tort law's basis showed. Justice Cardozo concluded in *MacPherson* that where "injury to persons" "is to be foreseen," "foresight of the consequences involves the creation of a duty." Yet neither Professor Bohlen nor Justice Cardozo stated the basis for that tort-law duty. The boldness of Justice Cardozo's statement hid the uncertain ground he gave it. Beware justices writing grandly.

Commentators call 20th-century products-liability law a revolution, even though the ancients had something much like products liability for at least boats, walls, and houses. Yet the products liability cases that followed *MacPherson* had its same failing that they did not clearly articulate the basis for extending products liability. Not long after *MacPherson*, Justice Herman wrote in the seminal 1932 case *Baxter v Ford Motor Co.* of "[t]he vital principle" upholding his court's decision to extend products liability beyond express-warranty actions. Even though Justice Herman wrote of the need that tort law rules "square with justice" and "meet the full intendment of the law," Justice Herman did not articulate the vital principle or aspect of justice with which law must square, or the full intendment of the law to which he referred. The products-liability revolution was underway without articulated basis.

In the same progression after *MacPherson* and *Baxter*, Justice Francis in 1960 in another seminal case *Henningsen v Bloomfield Motors, Inc.*, extended implied-warranty theories for products liability. In doing so, Justice Francis referred to the "transcendent value" of this extension of products liability, how "[a]n instinctively felt sense of justice cries out against" limitations on that liability, and how "[t]he task of the judiciary is to administer the spirit as well as the letter of the law." Claiming *transcendence* is not articulating basis, particularly when writer does not state that to which law now transcends. Nor is *instinct* or *spirit* enough to justify law, particularly when writer does not describe the instinct or spirit. *MacPherson, Baxter,* and *Henningsen* each saw the need for stating firm grounds justifying the existence and extension of tort law but at the opportune moment drew back. Tort law accepted the premises established in *MacPherson, Baxter,* and *Henningsen* even if without articulated grounds or sources.

During these mid-20th-century developments, cost/benefit analysis introduced into tort law another invitation to error. In 1947 in *United States v Carroll Towing Co.*, Judge Learned Hand stated that tort liability should depend on the burden of adequate precautions being less than the probability of the wrong times the gravity of the loss, or in mathematical form, $B < P \times L$. The *Carroll Towing* case involved a barge breaking free to damage another barge, due to its owner having failed to attend to its mooring. The liability theory was that if the cost of hiring an attendant to watch the ropes (or a better attendant, evidence suggesting that the hired hand had gone ashore) would have been less than the cost of the damaged barge, reduced by the probability of the barge damage, then the owner should be liable. In an earlier 1940 case *Conway v O'Brien*, Judge Hand had stated the same formula in similar terms:

> The degree of care demanded of a person by an occasion is the resultant of three factors: the likelihood that his conduct will injure others, taken with the seriousness of the injury if it happens, and balanced against the interest which he must sacrifice to avoid the risk.

Judge Hand's utilitarian premise took hold. Scholars thereafter conceived of tort law's care as *burden* rather than opportunity to serve or duty to protect, and burden borne properly only with concomitant loss. Care not, the rule invited, unless not caring will cost. Utility tests became and remain a dominant model. The Restatement (Third) of Torts: Products Liability §2 adopts a risk-utility test for judging the defectiveness of a product. Scholars popularized Judge Hand's formula despite that Judge Hand warned in *Conway v O'Brien* that it was unworkable. Litigants could not measure at least two of its variables with satisfactory reliability or even theoretically, he concluded. Variety in artificial and natural circumstances makes estimating the probability of injury-causing events incredibly speculative. In his own words, the upshot of Judge Hand's speculation over a cost-benefit liability formula was simply to let the jury decide on their own standards:

> For this reason a solution always involves some preference, or choice between [] incommensurables, and it is consigned to a jury because their decision is thought most likely to accord with commonly accepted standards, real or fancied.

Good thing that juries would still get to decide because Judge Hand's formula was not only unworkable but fundamentally wrong. Any decently raised child could have told scholars that characterizing care as burden was a conceptual act straight out of hell. Above chapters show that care has for millennia been society's fundamental intrinsic value and organizing principle.

Care is not only duty but opportunity. Care's persistent exercise on behalf of family, friends, neighbors, customers, and clients carries with tangible and intangible rewards far beyond avoiding another's lawsuit due to loss. Yet Judge Hand's famous formula describes care as cost. Professor Bohlen made the same error equating care with "the loss sustained by the burden imposed upon the energies of him on whom the duty is laid...." "Care became the price of action," Professor Bohlen wrote, when to the contrary care has always been the cause for action.

From society and tort-law standpoints, describing autonomy, self-expression, or profit as benefit and care as burden may mean battle already lost. Law chooses sides already when placing autonomy, self-expression, or profit over care. All can benefit to the extent that they promote individual and social good. Yet only care does nothing but promote good, meaning that only care can be intrinsic end. Autonomy has its costs, as do self-expression and profit. For many torts, personal or corporate ends motivate the harmful conduct. We must measure autonomy, self-expression, and profit against deeper standards, to know where they must stop. The deepest standard is always care itself, the conscious, intelligent, effective, sensitive, and nuanced willing of good to others.

Can medical-device maker, whose mission is making products that heal, claim that an improved design preventing injury is burden and loss? Can physician, whose profession is to heal, claim that practices preventing injury are burden and cost? What happens when we view care of child, disabled spouse, or elderly parent as burden or loss? Care is the intrinsic saving value and liberating end, not cost on route to other ends. Only when viewing others as means rather than ends, and caring for others only when utilitarian rule compels, can one accept Judge Hand's formula. One can certainly consider the cost of a safety improvement to a product that already benefits users. Comparing safety's cost with other benefits to its absence remains a basic care equation, but shifting care to cost and burden injects foundational error. Once conceiving of care as burden, the next error comes more easily, which is to replace care with autonomy, self-expression, or profit as ultimate end, so that medical-device maker may profit selling unreasonably dangerous products.

Products liability's basis became more obscure with the materialist view that law has no ground or foundation and that judges have only pragmatic decisions to make in this case or that case for one or another party. Materialism's rejection of all prior foundations further obscured history, customs, sources, accepted grounds, and vital principles. The veiled references of Justices Cardozo, Herman, and Francis to ultimate sources, transcendent values, and justifying intent gave way to the Restatement (Second) of Torts §402A's product-centered risk-utility test.

Judge Richard Posner's 1990 opinion in *Indiana Harbor Belt R.R. Co. v American Cyanamid Co.* provides related strict-liability example. *Indiana Harbor* held that the shipper of a toxic chemical has no strict, ultra-hazardous activity liability for the toxin's having leaked free to contaminate railroad yard and threaten adjacent residential neighborhood. Judge Posner wrote that the inappropriate land use was residential living, admitting his own seeming brutality in so saying. Judge Posner readily accepted that a balloonist might be strictly liable for having crushed a gardener's tomatoes, as had been true in an older case, but not the toxic-chemical shipper for contaminating the yard. The *Indiana Harbor* opinion made no reference to justice, equity, proportion, care, vital principles, spirit of the law, or other intrinsic goods because (as shown below) the opinion writer believed in no transcendent qualities. Without justifying foundation, the *Indiana Harbor* analysis reached surprising and (the threatened residents must have felt) disappointing results. The opinion analogized that by choosing to live near the railroad yard rather than in distant suburb, the poor residents had as much as built their homes between O'Hare Airport's runways. Query whether the poor residents had any choice to live in the suburbs and whether the residences were there long before shippers started sending through toxic chemicals. The opinion made no reference to law's obligation to protect the poor who cannot protect themselves or to the value of their toxin-free lives.

Judge Posner, who is the most-cited of all law scholars, writes in *The Problematics of Moral and Legal Theory* that appeals to timeless principles "spurious" because no such principles exist. His materialist view that no principle and only colliding atoms exist is itself an a priori assumption. If he were correct, then how, not having any referential standpoint, could he even tell? Our conscious minds, cognizant of the equal consciousness of others, inevitably face us with the reality of objectivity, of an independent plain. Materialism's denial depends on the very objectivity and independence that it denies because without standpoint to deny one can make no meaningful denial. The point is not that *Indiana Harbor* was wrong but that its writer made no effort to justify the decision on tort law's fundamental ground, the writer believing that no ground exists. The opinion's sarcasm and incivility toward plaintiff's counsel and trial judge, and acknowledged brutality, seeming unfairness, and loose analogies, confirm its unmoored state.

Other contemporary writings on tort law's ground or basis fail to articulate anything more satisfying than the above tautologies and ciphering. In 1993, Owen published in the Notre Dame Law Review an article *The Moral Foundations of Products Liability Law: Toward First Principles*. The article surmises that the foundation of products-liability law lies in individual freedom as the "most fundamental, and most important, moral and political value" placing "responsibility upon each person to plan and live a life that is 'good' for that individual...." The article concludes that a person's acts are morally right if perfecting of that person's capacities, leading to the fulfillment of that person's personality. The argument that duties of care lie in freedom to fulfill oneself is more than problematic. Tort law cannot ground its duty of care for one another on one's free pursuit of one's own personality. Indeed the argument begs the question, freedom from what other than the care that tort law imposes? Individual pursuit of personal fulfillment at the expense of care for others is more cause rather than panacea for reckless, negligent, or otherwise harmful conduct. The Restatement (Second) of Torts §291 acknowledges that negligence begins when "a reasonable man would recognize [the act in question] as involving a risk of harm to another."

The list of self-fulfilling torts is long including the outrage arising when the *Akers v Alvey* defendant pursued intense sexual desires, assault and battery arising when the *Doe v Hartz* defendant tried to satisfy his sexual desires, defamation committed when the *Neiman-Marcus v Lait* defendant pursued his salacious writing, conspiracy committed when the *Commercial Business Systems v Bellsouth Services* defendant's greed made him take a bribe, or negligence committed when the *Bierczynski v Rogers* defendant pursued the thrill of a street drag race. The duty of care involves reasonable self-control, limits to personal freedom, not its fulfillment. Scholars cannot ground tort law's other-centered duty of care in self-pursuing freedom, even though doing so would satisfy a *me* generation.

Tort law needs no ground extrinsic to care to justify its rules. Justification must lie in something intrinsic to be justification. Statements requiring reference to something else are not ground or justification. Tort law need not prove itself efficient, for instance, because care (welfare or good to being) justifies efficiency. Efficiency has no intrinsic value. It also has no greater value than any other tort-law rationale because all rationales seek the same intrinsic end, which is to care, meaning to promote human welfare. Though utility tests are common in tort law, so representative of this materialist age putting thing before person and relationship, utility is like efficiency not justification. Utility, or usefulness, must serve some other end, asking useful to what? The utility of an act or product lies in its tendency to promote the good of those whom the act or product serves. To measure utility, we must ask whether the intentions of manufacturing product are consistent with attributes of care, not whether the product has independent usefulness. Utility can become an end, but its doing so would be distortion worthy of parody. Cars without seatbelts still have tremendous utility. Tort law does not require care because care has utility. Rather, we must know what it means to care even to be able to conceive of utility.

Do not miss this conclusion's consistency with world-historical experience. To conclude that care to universal being is all interaction's intrinsic end is to say neither more nor less than that which philosophers and theologians have long said, every commandment hanging on that commandment. Scholar Sherwin calls it law's beatitude, bending Nietzsche's will to power into law's redemptive justice. With care so plainly at the center of civil liability, tort law need not refer or defer to profound teachings and traditions to accept care as tort law's intrinsic end. Yet law also need not deny that those teachings and traditions exist as another reflection of the care that law must recognize. Lawyer-theologian Finney and contemporaries influenced abolition of flogging, slavery, and cruelty to women, children, and animals, and supported other profound legal reforms. Law can take as encouragement that first-order theorists and saints have for millennia accepted regard for universal being as justifying end. Care is no modern tort-law invention but rather ancient edict facing modern challenge from self-centered materialist viewpoint. Tort law demands that we put others with ourselves, whereas modern viewpoint puts self before others. Tort law is precisely where self-seeking autonomy ends.

Chapter 10

Lawlessness Revealed

The Supreme Court has in one line of recent tort-law cases put self-fulfilling autonomy right where *care* should be. It did not start that way. With what Chief Justice Rehnquist labelled his "customary clarity," Justice Stewart in the 1966 defamation case *Rosenblatt v Baer* put tort law's basis right where it has always been:

> The right of a man to the protection of his own reputation from unjustified invasion and wrongful hurt reflects no more than our basic concept of the essential dignity and worth of every human being—a concept at the root of any decent system of ordered liberty.

The "concept" both "basic" to and "the root of" tort law's ordered liberty is none other than "the essential" "worth" of each of us. Tort laws knows each individual's intrinsic value. Tort law *cares,* and for each of us, not for efficiency, autonomy, or self-expression, although those things have value when promoting care for individual lives. Tort law's duty of care promoting good to each of us has justification because each of us has worth beyond measure of other things we value. Law must constrain us to respect one another's value. Nations have slaughtered tens of millions in genocide over the past 120 years precisely because their lawmakers did not value lives equally. A being's value is as undeniable to law as to medicine, art, literature, philosophy, theology, and any other pursuit or profession. Charity,

153

benevolence, or simply good to being root tort law as surely as any other field.

Yet two more-recent Supreme Court cases rejected care as tort law's intrinsic good and foundation in favor of freedom as the intrinsic good. The first case *Bose Corp. v Consumers Union* protected false commercial expression with the Court saying that "the freedom to speak one's mind is ... a good unto itself...." The second case *Hustler Magazine v Falwell* protected an intentionally severely distressing pornographic depiction, quoting *Bose Corp.* and repeating that "the freedom to speak one's mind is ... a good unto itself...." Even within tort law, the law of care, the Supreme Court conceives of expression as an ultimate or intrinsic rather than instrumental or conditional good, just as it did in later grounding rights in "transcendent" "autonomy." The modern Court favors self-expression and personal freedom as fundamental values over the care that tort law would otherwise require of us for one another. The Court's higher rule is "do for yourself" rather than "do to others as you would have done for yourself."

Self-definition over constraints respecting others are hardly new. Man's primal act was to choose his own rules over those of supremely caring God. Freedom forever challenges us. Yet the will to choose paths is a necessary ingredient in determining the value of any. In few cases did freedom show both its sides so clearly than in the Supreme Court's *Hustler Magazine v Falwell*. The defendant porn-magazine publisher Flynt fabricated as purposeful, disgusting, and injuring an attack on reputation as imagination could muster. Commentators reach different conclusions about the Court's *Hustler Magazine* outcome. For our purposes, though, the case reveals most clearly the Court's underlying premise that freedom is a "good unto itself."

This chapter explores what scholars mean when defining *intrinsic good*. Despite the Court's *Hustler Magazine* assertion, freedom is not good unto itself but rather conditional good. Freedom is as much an attribute of murder, mayhem, and other vices as of virtues like care and its corollaries. This chapter shows that law must regard freedom as conditional rather than intrinsic good. Constitutional-law scholar Robert Post attributes the current disarray in the Court's First Amendment jurisprudence to precisely that error, although here we address tort rather than constitutional law. This chapter also addresses the argument that freedom should balance and the overriding of tort law's care. The chapter concludes that law should regard freedom not as opposed to care but rather found in care as freedom's author.

First though, consider the argument that freedom is indeed the prime good. In both *Bose Corp.* and *Hustler Magazine,* the Supreme Court declared speaking one's mind to be an intrinsic good. A reader need not parse the Court's opinions to reach that conclusion, for the Court said so itself. When the Court equated speaking one's mind with an intrinsic good, it included speaking one's mind intending to destroy another because that was *Hustler Magazine's* factual context. Flynt had testified on deposition that his purpose in publishing that Falwell had sexual intercourse with his mother in an outhouse was to "assassinate" Falwell, meaning to destroy and silence him. The *Hustler Magazine* decision may not have depended on the Court's intrinsic-good assertion. The Court could instead have relied on instrumental justifications (the search for truth through parody, for example) for its outcome, in line with existing free-speech doctrine.

Yet in its freedom-as-ultimate-good argument, the Court was pursuing a broader theme, not just deciding single cases. The last chapter showed the Court employing the same freedom-as-ultimate-good theme in autonomy's "transcendent dimension." The Court has a history of seeing self-realization as transcendent value, beginning in *Whitney v California* when Justice Brandeis labeled freedom to be "both ... an end and ... a means." Justice Brandeis later added that freedom's end was "to make men free to develop their faculties" for the "discovery and spread of political truth," making freedom sound more means.

Self-realization as an end got a boost from the Court's desegregation case *Brown v Board of Education* when the Court accepted lawyer Thurgood Marshall's assertion that self-identification has independent value. Twenty years later, Justice Marshall in the prisoner-rights case *Procunier v Martinez* raised

155

self-expression first to a "need" and then to a "demand" and "basic yearning[]" of the "human spirit," holding, "When the prison gates slam behind an inmate," that inmate's "quest for self-realization" has not "concluded." The same year, the Court decided *Spence v Washington* holding in essence that speech's value was in speech itself rather than message or context. The *Spence* test was so broad that scholar Post marveled at how "transparently and manifestly false" it was, but the test survived and prospered. Self-realization got another boost when the Court later wrote in *Hurley* that "the fundamental rule of protection under the First Amendment" is "that a speaker has the autonomy to choose the content of his own message." Autonomy now justified speech, not democratic truth-seeking. When *Procunier* acknowledged the "demand" and "basic yearning[]" of the "human spirit" for self-expression, the Court made the human spirit law's arbiter over the supreme Spirit's care we once owed one another.

Scholars found outside of law substantial and growing literature on the self to support the Supreme Court's self-realization spirit. Murchison wrote that "[l]aw's interest appears to be the individual's process of self-forgetting in the undertaking of action...." Emerson held that law's end was to aid individuals in realizing their own character. Redish held "individual self-realization" as the First Amendment's "one true value," rooted in individual self-determination and self-development. Schauer acknowledged that the self-realization value means speech unfettered by others. Law was accepting autonomy as prime organizing principle and transcendent value.

The autonomy argument claims so much as to be meaningless. The Supreme Court's *Hustler Magazine* reference to an intrinsic good might a reader recall Plato for whom justice was an intrinsic good, justice requiring no conditions for justification. To appreciate conceptual difficulties the Court's assertion presents, recall what the Court meant by a "good unto itself," something which is good without condition, qualification, or limitation. Attributes that are good only in certain circumstances are not intrinsic goods. Only goods without condition are goods unto themselves. As shown above, care and carelessness share attributes, liberty, intelligence, and effectiveness being some of them. Care and carelessness both depend on liberty in the ability to choose conduct, intelligence in knowledge of the character of choice, and effectiveness in bringing about a chosen end. The infamously depraved are so because they possess liberty to act, intelligence to understand the depravity of their act, and efficiency in having accomplished what they sought. Even so favored an attribute in our process-oriented law as *deliberation* is not good unto itself but merely a frequent ally (and occasional foe) to care. The conclusion depends on deliberation's purpose. Freedom is good only instrumentally and conditionally.

Freedom's conditional good is even so when the freedom exercised is self-expression. Scholar Post calls "doomed from the start" the Court's attempt to protect speech for speech's sake because "'speech as such' has no constitutional value...." Post concludes that "value inheres instead in specific forms of social order" just as "speech has tended to receive the constitutional protection necessary for it to facilitate the maintenance and success of specific forms of social order." Similarly, scholar Robert George calls expression's value solely instrumental: "Speech that fails to advance any human good is valueless, for the value of speech is instrumental, not intrinsic...." Consider a gorgeous aria of excruciating poignancy. If the leader of the world's most powerful nation sang it as sole response to genocidal regime's murder of hundreds of thousands, then sound minds would call that aria an abomination. Genocide requires as response military commands, not arias. Even implying art or aesthetic in self-expression again makes expression instrumental rather than inherently valuable. When encountering a person dying of starvation, the appropriate response is to feed the person, not to paint a beautiful picture of hunger. Painting may raise conscience and publicity to help the hungry, but helpfulness depends on skill and contacts of the painter, again making painting instrumental rather than intrinsic. One cannot prove intrinsic the goodness of self-expression.

Labeling freedom "self-realization" or "self-fulfillment" does not justify it as ultimate. As Post shows, realization and fulfillment are social practices that, like other social practices, have "appropriate time and place." The doctor who for self-realization diverts from accepted medical practice injuring the patient does not accomplish intrinsic good and deserves no legal protection. The lawyer who uses the courtroom for self-realization or the employee who uses the workplace for self-fulfillment are hardly justified. Tape Flynt's pornographic parody of Falwell to an employee's locker, and law would recognize a strong case of sexual harassment. Self-fulfillment and self-realization are like freedom only conditional goods. Sophism glorifies self-expression as principle apart from and deeper than freedom. An advocate can call anything self-expressive. To call painting expression but skilled kitchen labor something less is probably cultural arrogance. Indeed is anyone more or less self-expressive than another? Self-expression is not gift to bourgeoisie but necessity for all of us at every moment.

The question of freedom's nature turns one to asking *what are freedoms for?* Garvey's book of that title concludes that freedom's value depends on whether one exercises it for good ends. "There is no general right to freedom ... only particular freedoms," he writes in reference to free speech, press, religion, and assembly. Even within particular freedoms, law exempts from protection whole categories such as malicious defamation, bribes, and obscenity. Garvey inverts liberalism's first principle "that the right is prior to the good" so as to "begin with an idea about what is good to do, and then assign rights so as to allow people to do what is good." Garvey concludes that autonomy does not justify freedoms. On the other hand, when Garvey concludes that "the pursuit of knowledge" "is intrinsically good" and "worth doing for its own sake," he makes the same error. Knowledge of evil, such as how to hire a hit man, destroy a marriage, or abuse a child, is not something to desire. Garvey himself gives a frightening example in the extraordinary success of Nazi propaganda among educated and rational people. Pursuit of knowledge is no intrinsic good.

The good news of the Court seeking intrinsic goods is the effort, not the Court's mistaken conclusion. Law continues to face philosophical divide between pragmatic materialists holding no ideal or standard and others who see ideals and standards as more real than imagined and their rejection cause of increasing dysfunction. In its freedom-as-intrinsic-good quips, the Supreme Court tried to underpin the materialist's self-actualizing worldview with Platonic ideal, uneasy union at best. The Court could have chosen truth, justice, care, or other goods when it instead chose the oft-injuring freedom. Yet seeking good has its own value. Citing extensive writing by Charles Taylor on the self while hoping for new direction to self-realization law models, Murchison argues that self-realizing "spurs a greater awareness of the world" possibly "in the direction of justice," especially if each person's "moral strength" "flourish[es]" for the "betterment of society." Self-fulfillment as moral ideal could promote justice. We discover transcendent meaning independent of self through inward articulations and outward expressions.

Cognitive expression, even an infant's first word, may have something of inherent value in transcending self. Thorough-going self-seekers would assert expression's ultimate meaning without any self-transcending. The Supreme Court projects self transcending authority to reach autonomous dimension, perhaps as scholar Bradley suggests in a sort of grand bargain, "We will be your Court, and you will be our people." By contrast, Taylor has self transcend *itself* to recognize moral authority against what Murchison calls "a background of external goods." Taylor does so to cure prevalent but debased and superficial experiments in self-fulfillment in "non-moral desire to do what one wants without interference." Taylor may indeed be on to something when writing of transcending rather than fulfilling self because as the old saints say, the greatest victory one can have is over one's self.

Law needs such a victory. Post calls the Court's definitional attempts "failures of judicial craftsmanship of truly stunning proportions." Their results are equally hard to stomach, and not only in *Bose Corp.* protecting fraudulent commercial speech and the *Hustler Magazine* decision protecting severely distressing publication intended to destroy. Following *Hustler Magazine*, the Court in *The Florida Star v B.J.F.* concluded a series of cases undermining tort law's privacy protection in favor of expression. *The Florida Star* decision allowed the press to publish a rape victim's name in violation of state law, even though the publication's foreseeable results included repeated rape threats, flight from home under police protection, and counseling for severe distress. After the decision cited no value to the rape disclosure, stated no limit to expression, and acknowledged no basis for tort law's privacy, the Court's dissenters concluded, "Today, we hit the bottom of the slippery slope."

The tort-case context in which the Court has declared freedom an intrinsic good is important. The Court pits freedom not against arbitrary or paternalistic state regulation but against care. At stake in these tort cases was personal wellbeing and, moreover, how one should relate to another as to the other's wellbeing. If the Court had called freedom an intrinsic good in cases involving direct state regulation of speech, one would explore the regulation's purpose for justification on that other side of the ledger. The Court's assertion of freedom as intrinsic good in tort cases put the Court's transcendent freedom above care for others.

Tort law has long balanced care against freedom. Yet scholars further assert not just balance but competition between care and freedom, as if one must inevitably limit the other. Post writes that "privacy torts limit individual liberty," while Keating summarizes the "task of tort accident law" as "to reconcile our competing interests in liberty and security" in our daily business. Others see tort law as directly harmful to freedom. Geisfeld perceives that "[a]ny precautionary obligations tort law imposes ... would also be detrimental to [the] liberty interests" we exercise. Others even see freedom as the author of care such that tort law has its justification in liberty. Wright suggests in a collection of leading tort law writers that individual freedom justifies tort law, an assertion opposite the truth, which is that liberty depends on our showing a reasonable degree of care toward one another.

Logic should have us question that freedom and care require competitive balancing. Garvey gave us an important corollary to his thesis that freedom is no universal right. Even where freedom does exist as fundamental right, the freedom may not be bilateral freedom to either do or not do what one wants. Bilateral freedoms exist, even having benefit of apparent even-handedness. The right to practice a certain religion reasonably implies right to practice no religion. Yet liberty of the North to prohibit slavery does not imply liberty of the South to allow it. Garvey rightly characterizes the Constitution's nearly fatal compromise on that issue as "failure to pursue good and forbid evil ... at the level of fundamental principles...." That law must make judgments concerning good and evil puts the houses of care and freedom in order and at peace with one another. One has no freedom to murder. Care and freedom are not competitors but companions.

Post sees other problems with judicial balancing of liberty interests. Cases do not assign rights and interests but rather authorize social practices in certain settings. In cases like *Pickering v Board of Education* and *U.S. v National Treasury Employees*, the Supreme Court rejected balancing anything. Balancing implies muddled compromise of substantial interests when courts instead hope to authorize internally logical and coherent social practices. Balancing tests abstract interests from the social settings that lend them their meaning. Post concludes that "we cannot ever write on a clean slate, as though legal values and interests simply fell disembodied from a clear sky," and that purporting to enables courts to skirt pertinent social dimensions.

The difficulty of balancing grows acute when the Court assigns one consideration, freedom, intrinsic-good status. When one interest has intrinsic value, opposing interests stand no chance of outweighing it. Intrinsic goods have no instrumental equal, making balancing impossible. *The Florida Star v B.J.F.* proves this conceptual conundrum. When the defendant newspaper unlawfully published the plaintiff rape victim's name, the publication resulted in the unidentified rapist's death threats against the victim, requiring the victim to move and hide with police protection, and receive counseling for distress. In dissenting Justice White's words quoting the Supreme Court case *Coker v Georgia*, the victim's interest was to protect herself against what "[s]hort of homicide ... is the 'ultimate violation of self.'" The victim had huge interest, for the violation of which a jury awarded $100,000. Yet, *The Florida Star* majority found little to weigh in her favor when reversing the verdict. Decrying the Court's absolutist position, Justice White asked for at least some balancing "in a civilized and humane society." Balancing though is the problem. Civilized society, meaning a modicum of care, stands no chance with freedom as intrinsic good and self-expression as fundamental value.

Prior chapters have shown that the universal ethic of care for one another has always been tort law's intrinsic basis. Could care authorize liberty? The Court in its more-sensible moments has concluded something like it, particularly when Justice Stewart concurred in *Rosenblatt v Baer* that "[t]he right of a man to the protection of his own reputation" from harm "reflects no more than our basic concept of the essential dignity and worth of every human being." Justice Stewart immediately echoed that the "concept [is] at the root of any decent system of ordered liberty." Liberty begins with care. Justice Stewart's insight was the dissenters' refrain in a series of Supreme Court tort cases in which freedom advanced and care retreated, dissenters quoting his *Rosenblatt* dissent in *Time, Inc. v Hill*, *Rosenbloom v Metromedia*, *Paul v Davis*, and *Time, Inc. v Firestone*.

Although it makes a good one, care may not be the only intrinsic good that law promotes. Answering his own question *What are freedoms for?* Garvey suggests that law protects freedom of religion because exercise of religion is good unto itself. For adherents, religion is good unto itself because God commands it, meaning that one owes transcendent duty to comply without instrumental justification. That adherence glorifies God is wholly sufficient. Religion can also be instrumental good to the extent that its practice promotes life, peace, health, truth, care, and wellbeing. Some acts taken in the name of religion have not been good. Yet so too, many legislative and individual acts, taken in the name of good, have turned out not at all to be so.

Similarly, if one distinguishes devotion to care from the particular acts one unwisely chooses to represent that devotion, then logic eliminates or diminishes the problem. Care has nothing wrong it, ever, even though we are often wrong in how we choose to express it. We are not perfect or omniscient but rather continuously subject to the biases and other distortions that come with our peculiar subjectivity and self-interest. So too with religion, that if one distinguishes devotion to universal being from particular acts of devotion, then devotion is indeed intrinsically good notwithstanding that particular devotional manifestations, such as the sacrifice of a child or an entire religious community (thinking of Jonestown), would not be good at all but instead represent a contrary condition.

So what then is freedom's proper place relative to care? Freedom must in its essence be freedom *from* something, or it is not freedom. Language defines freedom as the absence of some form of constraint. The mistake that the Court and scholars make is to conceive of freedom as freedom from *care*. Do all the balancing you want, but freedom from care in no sense defines freedom or justifies case outcomes. Constantly or frequently acting without care in no sense makes one more free and indeed is likely to accomplish the opposite. Nor do we define freedom as freedom from *want* (meaning from desire). We can be perfectly free in law's sense but remain in great need of a good meal, that is, be quite unhappily hungry. Rather, freedom consists of freedom from *carelessness*, meaning freedom from *wrong*, freedom from *selfishness*, freedom from *greed*, and freedom from those other things that we know to motivate hate, ill will, malice, and other forms of carelessness.

We use the word *freedom* in two ways, and if law is to get its intrinsic goods right, then scholars must not confuse the two. In one respect, we say that we have the freedom to choose, and indeed we do. Will is innate to us, an essential and treasured aspect of our being. Yet we also have freedom to both enjoy and suffer consequences. To live consequentially is true freedom. Law should not remove from us our right to receive that which is due, whether good or bad, from our actions. Freedom to choose both implies and requires freedom to receive choice's consequence. We must not, as the Supreme Court's jurisprudence to some degree does, glorify freedom to choose without simultaneously honoring freedom to receive consequences. When the Supreme Court conceives of an arena for freedom to choose without the consequences, it creates an unsound, unreasonable, and unsustainable forum. It creates a jail, prison, or vacuum in which actions are without consequences, stealing from us not only enjoyable fruits of our labor but something worth far more to us, discipline for and correction of our wrongs.

Tort law's care limits freedom only by context. Physicians must conform their conduct to a community standard when treating patients, a community of physicians determining that standard. The physician's standard of care is not merely as to conduct but as to expression. A physician must obtain the patient's informed consent to treatment, not merely as to what physicians wish to express but also what patients wish to hear. The physician must convey information that the reasonable patient would want to hear regarding treatment risks and benefits. A physician has freedom to express the physician's self within those parameters and, indeed, *outside* of those parameters, in the latter case then being equally free to suffer court order to compensate the patient when undisclosed treatment risks injure the patient.

In that sense, tort law's rule of care is a law without limit, preserving perfect liberty to do that which reflects reasonable care. Drive your car within the speed limit and other rules of care as far, for as long, and in whatever direction you want. You have perfect liberty to drive within the speed limit, but you also have liberty to drive outside the speed limit with all its attendant consequence. We can always choose care or carelessness, having then the even greater liberty to receive the choice's consequences. Liberty to intentionally inflict emotional distress, defraud through commercial speech, or commit other torts but without consequences is not liberty at all, depriving us of consequence, discipline, and redemption that tort law so graciously offers. Liberty lies within consequence of care. Liberty in the positive normative sense describes social conduct having due consequence.

Libertine claims right of self-determination as intrinsic good, when self-determination is instead neutral fact. We do exactly as we wish with our minds and members, the fact of that self-determination having no bearing on evil or good. Goodness instead depends on the self-determination one adopts. Determine yourself as Jeffery Dahmer did, sexually abusing, torturing, murdering, and eating children, and none will call that good. Extremes are good teachers. Economist might say that some value liberty more than others, making choice the intrinsic good. The argument presumes limit on value, each having only so much coin with which to value, when to the contrary each of us values without limit. Economist may presume that only those who have real coin should participate in the valuing process. Judge Posner's essay on the foundation of tort law asserts that the poor are not able to buy even clean air to breathe, leaving him to "prescind" from this "baseline problem."

Let us not prescind but instead cure baseline problems. Take the example of the epicurean who claims to "value" food taste so highly that he spends his last dollar on a sumptuous meal rather than tithing, caring for his family, or doing the other sensible things which fulfill responsibilities, care for ourselves and others, and lend balance to a life. The libertine and economist might claim that such is the nature of choice and of liberty that the epicurean ought in an efficient market to have that freedom to value food taste – that to the epicurean, sensuality is the balance. But who is to say that the one who tithes and feeds his family rather than buying the lavish meal values food taste any less? Indeed in truth he may value it much more than the epicurean but believe only that the simple meal he will eat with his family knowing that his other obligations are met will taste far better than anything the epicurean could purchase. He who has found in care that perfect law of liberty has valued and purchased without limit. There is no limit to the coin of value. To solve Judge Posner's baseline problem, the poor man values his breath as much as the rich man who would deny it to him. Indeed he who would refuse to deny it to another may value it far more. To conceive of the value we place on one another or on that activity in which we engage as a limited market is a fundamental misconception. What one discovers (which history itself has taught us) is instead that these things have no limits.

Thus care is, or is an essential aspect of, that perfect law which authorizes liberty. The one who follows that perfect law has liberty indeed. Where the good sense of care is, there also is perfect freedom. That which constrains is not the duty (it should almost be said the opportunity) of care so much as it is the commission of contrary, harmful acts. Constraint and bondage come not from caring for one another or even (thinking of comparative negligence doctrine) from caring for ourselves, but rather from failing to care. It is precisely when we abandon care as the perfect law of liberty that we become enslaved to the consequences (legal, personal, and otherwise) of carelessness. The contrary myth that care constrains liberty, or still worse, that liberty is set against and constrains care, fundamentally misunderstands both law of care and nature of liberty. Yet that is where the Supreme Court has pointed us. We need to recover and preserve tort law's ground in care.

Conclusion:
Who Cares?

One figure used by those who want to see further changes in American tort law, to justify those changes, is that the national economy incurs an annual $246 billion *tort tax*. Reform advocates say that the figure is the total of every cost associated with any form of accident insurance or compensation, not only tort-liability payments to plaintiffs in, say, motor-vehicle negligence actions but also worker's compensation payments for workplace injuries not necessarily arising out of anyone's fault, disability payments, and also insurance company expenses including not only the insurance adjuster's wages and defense counsel's fees but also the wages and bonuses earned by insurance company executives. What is the relative size of that *tax*? The national economy is about $17 trillion, and so the $246 billion "tort tax" figure is about one-and-a-half percent.

One way to look at that figure is that we spend about one-and-a-half cents out of every dollar going back to fix what we have broken. Think of the last home repair you undertook. You may have cut a piece of lumber a little short and had to go buy another piece, increasing the cost of the project by one-and-a-half percent. Would you instead just leave that part of the project unfinished? Or you may not have quite known what you were doing, and so you had to go back and do part of the project over again, making the project take one-and-a-half-percent longer. Would you instead just leave the last part of the project unfinished? Or maybe you cut your finger along the way. Would you just leave it without bandage and bleeding? One-and-a-half percent of fixing what we do does not seem unreasonable.

Is it really a *tax*? The money that the tort system spends is part of the private national economy. Doctors and other care providers who treat our injured, insurance-company employees who adjust and pay those costs, and lawyers who advocate for and against them, are also consumers. The wages they earn go to buy goods and services in the same proportion as others use their earnings to buy goods and services. The tort system looks less like a tax than another part of the economy. Then consider the *tax* if we do not compensate for injury and loss. The victim then bears the loss. The loss remains, although no system allocates and compensates it. Repair of damaged goods and rehabilitation of damaged lives are not possible or are less possible. Society just leaves more people and things behind, not participating in and promoting the national economy.

Commentators like Professors Nolan and Ursin in the Wayne Law Review say that we are "witnessing a reinvigoration of the no-fault idea, with scholars from across a broad ideological and scholarly spectrum supporting a variety of no-fault proposals." Michigan for instance has been a tort-reform battleground, so much so that the State Bar of Michigan began a 2004 Strategic Plan with a list of key assumptions that included that "[b]y 2006 lawyers in Michigan will have a no-fault tort system." Michigan already has worker's compensation and motor vehicle no-fault tort systems, both of which have been around for decades. State Bar planners probably meant that Michigan would soon have more of a no-fault system than it then had. Michigan's Supreme Court subsequently altered or eliminated several traditional common-law tort doctrines, modifying Michigan's fault-based tort system. One tort-law text then summarized under the heading "Judicial politics" that Michigan's Supreme Court, "committed to reducing tort liability," "overturned long-standing" [tort law] precedents" in 25 cases in a three-year period.

The probability of predictions of this sort taking place, or indeed the extent to which fundamental changes have already occurred, is not the final point. Instead, more of us who claim to know something about tort law, either by education or practice, should be asking whether abolition of fault-based tort law would be good or bad thing. What would the abolition of fault as a basis for tort law mean? Though political and industry influences may have more today to do with whether tort law retains a fault basis, tort-law practitioners should have something to say in the matter, especially when bar leaders see reform as key development likely to affect law practice. Before we get too excited about the anticipated dawn of a new age of fault-free tort law, we should look closer at what the light of that dawn may bring.

The above chapters show the misconception taught in law school that fault-based tort law is a modern development arising out of an early English common law where torts, to the limited extent they existed, were strict liability rather than fault based. That view is the only view taught among five leading tort casebooks including the venerable Prosser. That view suggests that tort-law reforms shifting the burden of accidental injury to the injured push the pendulum back toward a historical state in which tort law provided only piecemeal, occasional, and even anomalous remedy. The view supposes that tort law has reached beyond its zenith, our modern compassion and sensitivity to wrong having swung the pendulum too far in favor of the injured. Modern society's unusually diverse, discrete, and competitive interests probably also contribute to the seeming pervasiveness of today's tort law.

The above chapters also showed the history of fault in tort law, and not the history that most think. Among the very earliest of recorded and surviving old English cases, *I de S et ux. v W de S* from the year 1348, already had in it a rule of fault-based liability. The case held that an assault without battery was nonetheless compensable. Far beyond that old English case, the earliest of recorded laws, the ancient Laws of Ur-Nammu, Code of Lipit-Ishtar, Laws of Eshnunna, and Code of Hammurabi, all around 4,000 years old, each included fault-based liability provisions. The ancient Roman laws, including the famous Twelve Tables of 433

A.D., were replete with detailed fault-based tort liability provisions. And of course the Torah, which for millennia has been foundational text for Jews, Christians, and Muslims alike, contains fault-based rules for compensation. Taking as example admonitions to love God and your neighbor as you love yourself, tort law's rule of care is hardly recent invention. Commentators have long recognized care for one another to be a universal ethic, found in the world's major (and many of its minor) religions. Instead, the recent invention would seem to be that law does better without such moral. We are short-sighted to call the law of care, to call fault-based tort law, a recent development. That history is dubious at best.

Yet putting aside history (not by the way a wise thing to do), recent experience shows what tort law without fault might look like. Worker's compensation schemes do not depend on a finding of fault, compensating instead without respect to fault of employer or employee. Workplace injury is alone enough. Yet because the systems do not make liability depend on showing fault, the systems provide less deterrence to employers making worker injuries a cost of business. Compensation paid for the workplace death of an employee who had no financial dependents can be as little as a statutory $5,000 burial expense, leaving the grieving family without any judgment that careless wrong caused profound loss. Law justifies these systems by their substantial transactional saving, but worker's compensation systems still depend upon complex and specialized litigation procedures. Disputants do not litigate fault but do litigate causation, care, and expenses. The American Law Institute estimates worker's compensation payments to have risen from $1 billion in 1950 to nearly $35 billion in 1986 to $62 billion in 1992.

Results of eliminating fault have not been any clearer or more favorable in the instance of motor vehicle no-fault systems. Beginning in 1965 and over the next few years, 24 states and the District of Columbia had adopted such schemes. Several have since repealed them. By 2000 only 13 states had retained motor vehicle no-fault systems limiting access to the traditional tort system. The criticisms were that the motor vehicle no-fault systems were simply placing the burden of loss on the injured.

The expected gains by those who were not injured were not realized to the extent expected. Insurance rates were either not lower or were not so demonstrably lower as to warrant retention or expansion of the no-fault systems. No-fault reforms to tort law were proving more complex than they at first appeared.

Consider another, broader no-fault experience. In 1972 New Zealand adopted a general no-fault remedy for accidental injury, administered by the government and financed by vehicle, employer, and general taxation. New Zealand adopted a no-fault system not because of business or consumer movements but under labor-government legislation abolishing fault-based tort law. The philosophy was collective responsibility rather than individual responsibility, decidedly not American. According to the official Report of New Zealand's Royal Commission, the legislation was to be stop-over on the way to the perfect collective. One wonders whether such a tax-based, government-administered program would be consistent with American free-market and free-enterprise values. The labor source for New Zealand's tort reform suggests the irony that here in America business interests seem most willing to abandon capitalism for the pain market. New Zealand's no-fault scheme stood to undermine personal responsibility by removing fault from the public conscience. Participants came to view the scheme as unfair to non-wage earner accident victims including particularly women raising infant children, who were effectively subsidizing (by their uncompensated pain and suffering) accident costs.

Legislators introduced but rejected similar legislation in Australia. No other nation has such a no-fault system. New Zealand had dismal economic performance under its collectivist labor government, so much that a nationalist movement replaced the labor government. Hard to tell is the extent to which the no-fault system contributed to New Zealand's dismal economic performance. The New Zealand plan remains in effect today under the nationalist government but only in modified form in which risk insurance premiums have replaced social-welfare levies as the system's revenue and focus. That modified system should sound familiar to us for its resemblance to our own insurance system, even though the New Zealand system retained many features of no-fault.

Closer to home, Virginia and then Florida enacted medical-malpractice reforms altering recoveries for neurological injuries to newborns. Few claims arose under the former scheme, while the latter had problematic implementation under pressure to restore common-law liability principles. Commentators held that both schemes failed to achieve their no-fault goals, one of which was to attempt to deliver at least some new compensation to injured patients. These nascent no-fault schemes and other tort-reform legislation responded to doubling and then tripling of liability-insurance premiums in the mid-1980s, generally attributed to an explosion in tort claims. Yet according to an American Law Institute 1991 report, "more systematic analysis of trends has demonstrated either that there never was a true general explosion in tort litigation, or at least that any incipient trend has definitely subsided." A Harvard Medical Practice Study concluded that the great majority of medical-malpractice injuries do not result in tort claims.

Studies suggest the questionable character of no-fault tort law. Rand's Institute for Civil Justice published an empirical study on the effects of shifting from fault to no-fault in motor-vehicle liability. The report deduced that the total amount spent on compensating those injured by motor-vehicle accidents indeed went down by 22 percent in no-fault versus fault states. Yet the report also showed that no-fault systems accomplish that reduction by eliminating the injured person's non-economic recovery and reducing payment received by lawyers who serve the injured. The average amount received by the injured went down from $3,645 to $3,182. You can reduce insurance rates by eliminating recoveries and requiring the injured to bear the costs, but at some point we should ask whether requiring the injured to bear the costs is right. The Rand report concluded that a "generous" no-fault system "can have the opposite effect" of "increasing total injury coverage costs." The determinative question in system costs appears not to be whether the system is fault-based but rather the allowed recovery, or in other words the extent to which the injured should pay the price.

Debate also exists whether adoption of no-fault systems unwisely removes an appropriate deterrent to negligent conduct and increases accident rates. Do no-fault systems make for more dangerous workplaces and interstates? The deterrent effect of a no-fault system such as worker's compensation is uncertain because of the insurance industry's limited ability to discriminate between high and low risks and the litigation system's limited ability to distinguish (at least inexpensively) between meritorious and non-meritorious claims. Even under no-fault, the task of adjusting claims and rates remains hard and expensive work. Trying harder to distinguish, meaning to spend more money adjusting claims, defeats the purpose by externalizing rather than internalizing other costs, losing whatever deterrent effect adjusting premiums might achieve. Getting statistical answer on the level of deterrence is just too complicated. The only thing that does pretty clearly appear is that no-fault systems tend to make the non-negligent pay for the negligent.

Short of actual studies, a substantial commentary exists on the subject of fault versus no-fault tort law. Some commentators begin from the premise that injured persons making claims for compensation are "problems" and conclude that "[t]he only way to deal with" "higher costs" for both "smaller" and "larger" tort claims "is to get rid of claims for noneconomic damages in cases both large and small." The injured persons making those claims would doubtless disagree that they were the "problems" and might point instead to the negligent parties who injured them. Such is the influence of one's vantage point, either consumer advocating reducing insurance rates or injured person trying to keep the mortgage paid. We do well to keep in mind both perspectives and not too quickly take sides as to which is the better.

The most-interesting commentary is that advocating permitting individuals to choose between fault and no-fault systems, in motor-vehicle insurance coverage what goes by the *tort option*. Studies suggest that the tort option reduces insurance premiums for those who choose no-fault (thereby losing their traditional tort-law rights) but does not influence other rates for those who stick with the traditional fault system. Kentucky, New

Jersey, and Pennsylvania have adopted choice plans in somewhat different forms, warranting further study of those plans. The plans' advantage is not merely economic, meaning lower insurance premiums for those who choose fewer rights. The plans also preserve a substantial degree of both personal responsibility and choice.

Yet put these considerations aside a moment to ask whether one can really divorce fault from tort law. As this book began, the word *tort* comes from the Latin for twisted or French for injury. Tort lawyers know what it means, that injury to one occurred because of misconduct of another under conditions in which we expect compensation for the injury. A wrong done needs righting by wrongdoer (compelled by the law if necessary) to restore the one wronged. The above chapters show that compensation is an age-old question going back to the beginning of recorded law. The fighting questions are routinely the degree of care the wrongdoer owed the wronged and the amount of the compensation that would make good that wrong. On those scores, degree of care and amount of compensation, reform ought to continue as it has in the past, adapting to the peculiar technologies and expediencies of our time.

What cannot occur without tort law itself becoming twisted, losing justification and form, is to divorce care, that fundamental concept that we owe one another some regard, from tort law. We must recognize that care grounds tort law. Nothing has greater value than the human lives and capacities that tort law protects. Because nothing has greater value, law has no activity, rule, or purpose greater than to protect and promote those lives. Such is the ancient ethic to love our neighbor. Care likewise grounds tort law. As the law of care, tort law is an essential aspect of law generally. Law can do nothing greater than protect human life. Tort law's theoretical person of reasonable, ordinary, and due care, may be criticized character, but do not expect the reasonable person to break. Law simply cannot abandon care as prime components without losing all justification.

If in pursuing liberty or efficiency we throw out care for others, allowing dangerous vehicles driven dangerously on dangerous roads, causing more uncompensated carnage, we gain nothing. Liberty does not increase because injury destroys liberty of the injured. As to high insurance rates, law has a balance to strike, certainly to fight insurance fraud. Legislative and judicial reforms in that direction should continue but without making the mistake in thinking that insurance is pure cost. Insurance is instead caring for others in the common activities in which we engage that happen to cause injury. What ultimately lends meaning to our lives is not the speed at which we drive or quantity of goods we accumulate, or indeed the liberty in which we engage in conduct harmful to others, but care we show for one another along the way. Insurance sets aside a portion of our provision for those moments when our conduct is less than that which it should be in due care for others.

In the end, tort-law reforms can have their own ancient root in our tendency to put ourselves above others at others' cost. No wonder then that law in general and tort law in particular tend in the same disappointing direction. When care and service ethics wane in the culture, they wane both in the law profession and in law itself. As members of a profession founded on service to others in need, lawyers must not abandon their own tools, the tools of law, to desultory influences of culture. The profession should note motives when reshaping tort law, while remaining cognizant of both its historical role and fundamental value. Tort law cannot exist apart from care, just as we cannot exist apart from care, without cutting off the root of law and allowing law and life to wither. Strategic assumptions may be correct that care will soon be less a part of law than formerly, but we should continue to ask whether law, and whether we, will be any better off for care's absence.

As the Florida Supreme Court concluded in the tort case *Blackburn v Dorta*, "In the field of tort law, the most equitable result that can ever be reached by a court is the equation of liability with fault." Fault is obverse of care. Eliminating fault eliminates consideration of care, when care is a categorical imperative. Law cannot abandon care without losing all meaning and authority. The extent to which tort law reflects care by including fault as its basis is more a measure of us than measure of care's role or utility. We should treat the law of care, tort law, neither as annoyance nor modest fortuity but rather as a precious and essential commodity. Love harms no neighbor but instead fulfills the law.

Bibliography

Books and Articles:

ADDISON, C.G., A TREATISE ON THE LAW OF TORTS (1876).

Albeck, Shalom, *Torts*, in MENACHEM ELON, ED., THE PRINCIPLES OF JEWISH LAW 319 (1975).

Alexander, Mark C., *Don't Blame the Butterfly Ballot: Voter Confusion in Presidential Politics*, 13 STAN. L. & POL. REV. 121, 137 (2002).

American Bar Association, *Perceptions of the U.S. Justice System* 49 (1999), *reprinted in* 62 ALB. L. REV. 1307, 1320 (1999).

American Bar Association, Report of the Commission on the 21st Century Judiciary, *Justice in Jeopardy (Executive Summary)* 1 (2003).

Ames, James B., *Law and Morals*, 22 HARV. L.REV. 97, 113 (1908).

Ammar, Douglas B., *Forgiveness and the Law--A Redemptive Opportunity*, 27 FORDHAM URB. L.J. 1583, 1598 (2000).

Bedell, R. Patrick, *The Next Frontier in Tort Reform: Promoting the Financial Solvency of Nursing Homes*, 11 ELDER L.J. 361, 386 (2003).

BELL, PETER A., & JEFFREY O'CONNELL, ACCIDENTAL JUSTICE 182 (1997).

BEVEN, THOMAS, NEGLIGENCE IN LAW 21-22 (2nd ed. 1895).

Birks, Peter, *The Concept of a Civil Wrong*, in DAVID G. OWEN, EDITOR, THE PHILOSOPHICAL FOUNDATIONS OF TORT LAW 33 (1995).

Bohlen, Francis H., *The Basis of Affirmative Obligations in the Law of Tort*, 53 O.S./44 N.S. AM. L.REG. 209 (1905).

Borden, Diane L., *Invisible Plaintiffs: A Feminist Critique on the Rights of Private Individuals in the Wake of Hustler Magazine v. Falwell*, 35 GONZAGA L.REV. 291 (1999-2000).

Bottero, Jean, *How Sin Was Born*, in JEAN BOTTERO, ED., EVERYDAY LIFE IN ANCIENT MESOPOTAMIA 249-52 (2001).

Bovbjerg, Randall R., & Frank A. Sloan, *No-Fault for Medical Injury: Theory and Evidence*, 67 U.CINN. L.REV. 53, 102 (1998).

Bowbeer, Hildy, Todd A. Cavanaugh, & Larry S. Stewart, *Timmy Tumble v Cascade Bicycle Co.: A Hypothetical Case Under the Restatement (Third) Standard for Design Defect*, 30 U.MICH. J.L.REF. 511, 528-529 (1997).

Bradley, Gerard V., *The New Constitutional Covenant*, WORLD & I 374 (March 1994).

BUCKLAND, W.W., & ARNOLD D. MCNAIR, ROMAN LAW AND COMMON LAW: A COMPARISON IN OUTLINE 365 (2d ed. 1965) (original edition 1936).

BUDGE, E.A. WALLIS, BABYLONIAN LIFE AND HISTORY (1907).

Buell, Keith C., *"Start Spreading the News": Why Republishing Material from "Disreputable" News Reports Must Be Constitutionally Protected*, 75 N.Y.U. L.Rev. 966, 974 (2000).

Burmester, Byron F., *On Humanitarian Intervention: The New World Order and Wars to Preserve Human Rights*, 1994 UTAH L.REV. 269, 289 (1994).

Calabresi, Guido, *Does the Fault System Optimally Control Primary Accident Costs?*, 33 LAW & CONTEMP. PROB. 429 (1968).

Calabresi, Guido, *Some Thoughts on Risk Distribution and the Law of Torts*, 70 YALE L.J. 499 (1961).

CALABRESI, GUIDO, THE COSTS OF ACCIDENTS (1970).

Calabresi, Guido, *The Decision for Accidents: An Approach to Nonfault Allocation of Costs*, 78 HARV. L.REV. 713 (1965).

Calnan, Alan, *Ending the Punitive Damage Debate*, 45 DEPAUL L.REV. 101, 104 (1995).

CAMFIELD, BENJAMIN, THE COMPREHENSIVE RULE OF RIGHTEOUSNESS: DO AS YOU WOULD BE DONE BY 54-55 (1679)).

Carrington, Paul D., *The Common Thoughts of Men: The Law-Teaching and Judging of Thomas McIntyre Cooley*, 49 STAN. L.REV. 520 (1997).

Carrington, Paul D., & Adam R. Long, *The Independence and Democratic Accountability of the Supreme Court of Ohio*, 30 CAP. U. L.REV. 455 (2002).

Carroll, Stephen J., & James S. Kakalik, *No Fault Automobile Insurance: A Policy Perspective* vii (1991) (Rand: Institute for Civil Justice).

Carroll, Stephen J., James S. Kakalik, Nicholas M. Pace, & John L. Adams, *No-Fault Approaches to Compensating People Injured in Automobile Accidents* (1991) (R-4019-ICJ) (Institute for Civil Justice: Rand).

Casarez, Nicole B., *Examining the Evidence: Post-Verdict Interviews and the Jury System*, 25 HASTINGS COMM. & ENT. L.J. 499, 579 (2003).

Caudill, David S., *Post-Postmodern Redemptions of Self, Text, and Event*, 5 CARDOZO STUD. IN LAW & LIT. 143-58 (1993).

CHAFFEE JR., ZECHARIAH, FREE SPEECH IN THE UNITED STATES 33 (Antheum 1969) (1941).

Champagne, Anthony, *Television Ads in Judicial Campaigns*, 35 IND. L.REV. 669, 670 (2002).

Charrow, Robert P., & Veda R. Charrow, *Making Legal Language Understandable: A Psycholinguistic Study of Jury Instructions*, 79 COLUM. L. REV. 1306 (1979).

CHRISTIE, GEORGE C., JAMES E. MEEKS, ELLEN S. PRYOR, & JOSEPH SANDERS, CASES AND MATERIALS ON THE LAW OF TORTS 108 (4th ed. 2004).

Christie, George C., *The Uneasy Place of Principle in Tort Law*, in DAVID G. OWEN, EDITOR, THE PHILOSOPHICAL FOUNDATIONS OF TORT LAW 130 (1995).

Coase, Ronald, *The Problem of Social Cost*, 3 J.L. & ECON. 1, 8 (1960).

Coleman, Jules L., *The Practice of Corrective Justice*, in DAVID G. OWEN, EDITOR, THE PHILOSOPHICAL FOUNDATIONS OF TORT LAW 59 (1995).

Cook, Douglas H., *Negligence or Strict Liability? A Study in Biblical Tort Law*, 13 WHITTIER L.REV. 1, 7-12 (1992).

Cooley, Thomas M., *The Administration of Justice in the United States of America in Civil Cases*, 2 MICH. L.J. 341, 341-342 (1893).

Cummins, David J., Richard D. Phillips, & Mary A. Weiss, *The Incentive Effects of No-Fault Automobile Insurance*, 44 J. L. & ECON. 427 (2001).

Cutchin, James M., *The 1995 Illinois Civil Justice Reform Act: Has the Baby Been Thrown out with the Bath Water?*, 20 S. ILL. U. L.J. 117, 117 (1995).

Daube, David, *Direct and Indirect Causation in Biblical Law*, II VETUS TESTAMENTUM 246, 255 (1961).

DE COLQUHOUN, PATRICK M., 1 A SUMMARY OF THE ROMAN CIVIL LAW XI-XIV (1849).

DE COLQUHOUN, PATRICK M., 2 A SUMMARY OF THE ROMAN CIVIL LAW 457-461 (1849).

Delaney, Sarah K., *Stare Decisis v. the "New Majority": The Michigan Supreme Court's Practice of Overruling Precedent, 1998-2000*, 66 ALBANY L.REV. 871 (2003).

Diamond, Arthur S., *An Eye for an Eye*, 19 IRAQ 151 (1957).

DIAMOND, ARTHUR S., PRIMITIVE LAW: PAST AND PRESENT 47-48 (1971).

DOBBS, DAN B., THE LAW OF TORTS 25-27 (2000).

DOBBS, DAN B., & PAUL T. HAYDEN, TORTS AND COMPENSATION: PERSONAL ACCOUNTABILITY AND SOCIAL RESPONSIBILITY FOR INJURY 808-09, 820-22 (4th ed. 2001).

DRIVER, G.R., & JOHN C. MILES, 1 THE BABYLONIAN LAWS 408 (1952).

EDWARDS, CHILPERIC, THE HAMMURABI CODE 35-37, 62, 65-66, 70 (1904).

EDWARDS, CHILPERIC, THE OLDEST LAWS IN THE WORLD 6 (1906).

EHRENZWEIG, A., NEGLIGENCE WITHOUT FAULT (1951), *reprinted in* 54 CALIF. L.REV. 1422 (1966).

ELWORK, AMIRAM, ET AL., MAKING JURY INSTRUCTIONS UNDERSTANDABLE (1982).

Elwork, Amiram, et al., *Toward Understandable Jury Instructions, in* IN THE
JURY BOX: CONTROVERSIES IN THE COURTROOM 161, 176 (Lawrence S.
Wrightsman et al. eds., 1987)).

EMERSON, THOMAS I., THE SYSTEM OF FREEDOM OF EXPRESSION 6-7 (1970).

Emerson, Thomas I., *Toward a General Theory of the First Amendment*, 72
YALE L.J. 877, 879 (1963).

EMERSON, THOMAS I., TOWARD A GENERAL THEORY OF THE FIRST
AMENDMENT 3-7 (1966).

EPSTEIN, RICHARD A., TORTS 31-33, 385-86, 392-94.

FALK, ZE'EV W., HEBREW LAW IN BIBLICAL TIMES: AN INTRODUCTION 75
(2001).

Fein, Bruce, *Hustler Magazine v Falwell: A Mislitigated and Misreasoned
Case*, 30 WM. & MARY L.REV. 905 (1989).

Feldman, Heidi Li, *Prudence, Benevolence, and Negligence: Virtue Ethics
and Tort Law*, 74 CHI.-KENT L.REV. 1431, 1462 (2000).

FINKELSTEIN, J.J. THE OX THAT GORED (1981).

FINNEY, CHARLES G., SYSTEMATIC THEOLOGY 142-174 (1865).

FISH, STANLEY, THERE'S NO SUCH THING AS FREE SPEECH (1994).

FITZPATRICK-MCKINLEY, ANNE, THE TRANSFORMATION OF TORAH FROM
SCRIBAL ADVICE TO LAW 49 (1999).

FLEMING, JOHN G., THE LAW OF TORTS 9-14, 109 (7th ed. 1987).

Fletcher, George P., *Fairness and Utility in Tort Theory*, 85 HARV. L. REV.
537, 539-40 (1972).

Foster, Michael, *What Are Freedoms For? (Book Review)*, 48 Fed. Law. 85
(2001).

FRAZER, JAMES G., FOLK-LORE IN THE OLD TESTAMENT: STUDIES IN
COMPARATIVE LEGEND AND LAW 415-445 (1918).

Frech III, H.E., *State-Dependent Utility and the Tort System as Insurance:
Strict Liability Versus Negligence*, 14 INTERN. REV. OF LAW & ECON. 261,
268-269 (1994).

Galanter, Marc, *Real World Torts: An Antidote to Anecdote*, 55 MD. L. REV.
1093, 1103 n.28 (1996)).

Galt, Kimberly A., *The Need to Define "Care" in Pharmaceutical Care: An
Examination Across Research, Practice and Education*, 64 AM. J.
PHARMACEUTICAL EDUC. 223, 223-25 (2000).

GARVEY, JAMES H., WHAT ARE FREEDOMS FOR? (1996).

Geisfeld, Mark, *Negligence, Compensation, and the Coherence of Tort Law*, 91
GEO. L.J. 585, 592 (2003).

GEORGE, ROBERT P., MAKING MEN MORAL 195 (1993).

Giannetti, Matthew R., Note, *Circumcision and the American Academy of
Pediatrics: Should Scientific Misconduct Result in Trade Association
Liability?*, 85 IOWA L. REV. 1507, 1546 (2000).

Gjerdingen, Donald H., *The Politics of the Coase Theorem and Its Relationship to Modern Legal Thought*, 35 BUFF. L.REV. 871 (1986).

Goldberg, Deborah, et al., *The Justice at Stake Campaign, The New Politics of Judicial Elections* (2002).

Goldberg, John C.P., & Benjamin C. Zipursky, *The Moral of MacPherson*, 146 U.PA. L.REV. 1733, 1741 (1998).

Green, H. Marlow, *Common Law, Property Rights, and the Environment: A Comparative Analysis of Historical Developments in the United States and England and a Model for the Future*, 30 CORNELL INTL. L.J. 541, 544-546 (1997).

GREENAWALT, KENT, SPEECH, CRIME, AND THE USES OF LANGUAGE 57-60 (1989).

GROTIUS, HUGO, THE LAW OF WAR AND PEACE (1625).

GURNEY, O.R., THE MIDDLE BABYLONIAN LEGAL AND ECONOMIC TEXTS FROM UR (1983).

Haas, Dean J., *Falling Down on the Job: Worker's Compensation Shifts from a No-Fault to a Worker-Fault Paradigm*, 79 N. DAK. L.REV. 203, 205-06 (2003).

Harel, Alon, *Bigotry, Pornography, and the First Amendment: A Theory of Unprotected Speech*, 65 S.CAL.L.REV. 1887, 1896 (1992).

HARPER, FOWLER V., ET AL., 2 THE LAW OF TORTS 24, 377-78 (2d ed. 1986).

HARPER, FOWLER V., ET AL., 3 THE LAW OF TORTS 381-86 (2d ed. 1986).

Hemphill, Craig K., Note, *Smoke Screens and Mirrors; Don't Be Fooled Get the Economic Facts Behind Tort Reform and Punitive Damages Litigation*, 23 THURGOOD MARSHALL L.REV. 143, 168n.145 (1997).

Hittinger, Russell, *A Crisis of Legitimacy*, 44 LOYOLA L.REV. 83 (1998).

HOLMES, JR., OLIVER WENDELL, THE COMMON LAW iii-iv (1881).

Honore, Tony, *The Morality of Tort Law – Questions and Answers*, in DAVID G. OWEN, EDITOR, THE PHILOSOPHICAL FOUNDATIONS OF TORT LAW 59 (1995).

HOROWITZ, MORTON, TRANSFORMATION OF AMERICAN LAW, 1780-1860, 99-101 (1977).

Howell, Timothy D., *So Long "Sweetheart"-State Farm Fire & Casualty Co. v. Grandy Swings the Pendulum Further to the Right as the Latest in a Line of Setbacks for Texas Plaintiffs*, 29 ST. MARY'S L.J. 47, 49-50 (1997).

HUNTER, W.A., A SYSTEMATIC AND HISTORICAL EXPOSITION OF ROMAN LAW IN THE ORDER OF A CODE 16-17, 61 (4th ed. 1903).

Imwinkelried, Edward J., *Expert Testimony by Ethicists: What Should Be the Norm?*, 76 TEMP. L. REV. 91, 105 (2003).

Isaacs, Nathan, *Fault and Liability; Two Views of Legal Development*, 31 HARV. L.REV. 954, 955, 958-59, 963-67 (1918).

JACKSON, BERNARD S., STUDIES IN JUDAISM IN LATE ANTIQUITY; ESSAYS IN JEWISH AND COMPARATIVE LEGAL HISTORY 7 (1975).

Jackson, Bernard S., *Models in Legal History: The Case of Biblical Law*, 18 J. LAW & RELIGION 1, 3, 5 (2002-2003).

James, Jr., Fleming, *The Qualities of the Reasonable Man in Negligence Cases*, 16 MO. L. REV. 1 *passim* (1951).

JOSEPHUS, FLAVIUS, JEWISH ANTIQUITIES: BOOKS I-IV bk. IV, §280.

KANT, IMMANUEL, THE METAPHYSICAL ELEMENTS OF JUSTICE (1797).

Karsten, Peter, *Using One's Head: Were Jurists "Unconscious" Socio-Economic Ciphers or Conscious Agents? A Response to Friedman*, 24 LAW & SOC. INQUIRY 281, 288 (1999).

Keating, Gregory C., *Distributive and Corrective Justice in the Tort Law of Accidents*, 74 S. CAL. L.REV. 193, 197 (2000).

Keating, Gregory C., *Rawlsian Fairness and Regime Choice in the Law of Accidents*, 72 FORDHAM L.REV. 1857, 1858 (2004).

Keating, Gregory C., *Reasonableness and Rationality in Negligence Theory*, 48 STAN. L.REV. 311, 349-60 (1996).

Keeton, Robert, *Conditional Fault in the Law of Torts*, 72 HARV. L.REV. 401 (1959).

KEETON, ROBERT, & JEFFREY O'CONNELL, BASIC PROTECTION FOR THE ACCIDENT VICTIM (1965).

KEETON, ROBERT, LEWIS D. SARGENTICH, & GREGORY C. KEATING, TORT AND ACCIDENT LAW: CASES AND MATERIALS 283-85 (4th ed. 2004).

Kelley, Patrick J., & Laurel A. Wendt, *What Judges Tell Juries About Negligence: A Review of Pattern Jury Instructions*, 77 CHI.-KENT L. REV. 587, 590 592 (2002).

KELSEN, H., GENERAL THEORY OF LAW AND STATE 3 (1945).

Klayman, Elliott, & Seth Klayman, *Punitive Damages: Toward Torah Based Law Reform*, 23 CARDOZO L.REV. 221, 225 (2001).

KLUGER, RICHARD, SIMPLE JUSTICE 304-345 (Vintage 1977) (1975).

Korzec, Rebecca, *A Feminist View of American Elder Law*, 28 UNIV. TOLEDO L.REV. 547, 552 (1997).

Kramer, S.N., *The Ur-Nammu Law Code: Who Was its Author?*, 52 ORIENTALIA NS 453 (1983).

Lafont, Bertrand, *The Ordeal*, in JEAN BOTTERO, ED., EVERYDAY LIFE IN ANCIENT MESOPOTAMIA 201 (2001) (English translation).

Laguzza, James R., *Hustler Magazine, Inc. v. Falwell: Laugh or Cry, Public Figures Must Learn to Live with Satirical Criticism*, 16 PEPP. L.REV. 97 (1988).

Langvardt, Arlen W., *Stopping the End-Run by Public Plaintiffs: Falwell and the Refortification of Defamation Law's Constitutional Aspects*, 26 AM. BUS. L.J. 665 (1989).

Leininger, Madeline, *Foreword* to JEAN WATSON, NURSING: THE PHILOSOPHY AND SCIENCE OF CARING, at xi-xii (1979).

Lenga, J. Thomas, *The Golden Rule Still Applies*, 77 MICH. BAR.J. 1278 (1998).

Levmore, Saul, *Rethinking Comparative Law: Variety and Uniformity in Ancient and Modern Tort Law* 61 TUL. L.REV. 235, 240 (1986).

LIFTON, ROBERT JAY, THE PROTEAN SELF 28 (1993).

MAIN, HENRY S., ANCIENT LAW: ITS CONNECTION WITH THE EARLY HISTORY OF SOCIETY AND ITS RELATION TO MODERN IDEAS 15, 17-18 (1906).

MAIN, HENRY S., DISSERTATIONS ON EARLY LAW AND CUSTOM: CHIEFLY SELECTED FROM LECTURES DELIVERED AT OXFORD 5 (1886).

Malone, Wex S., *Ruminations on the Role of Fault in the History of the Common Law of Torts*, 31 LA. L.REV. 1, 27, 43 (1970).

MAITLAND, F., THE FORMS OF ACTION AT COMMON LAW 65 (1941).

McCarthy, David, *Rights, Explanation, and Risks*, 107 ETHICS 205, 212-15 (1997).

Mikhail, John, *Law, Science, and Morality: A Review of Richard Posner's* The Problematics of Moral and Legal Theory, 54 STAN. L. REV. 1057, 1086-87 (2002).

Miller, Richard S., *An Analysis and Critique of the 1992 Changes to New Zealand's Accident Compensation Scheme*, 5 CANTERBURY L.REV. 1 (1992) (also found at 52 MD. L.REV. 1070 (1993)).

Miller, Richard S., *The Future of New Zealand's Accident Compensation Scheme*, 11 U.HAW. L.REV. 1 (1989).

Miner, Roger J., *Judicial Ethics in the Twenty-First Century: Tracing the Trends*, 32 HOFSTRA L.REV. 1107 (2004).

Miner, Roger J., *Judicial Trends in the Twenty-First Century: Tracing the Trends*, 32 HOFSTRA L.REV. 1107 (2004).

Morris, Clarence, *The Relation of Criminal Statutes to Tort Liability*, 46 HARV.L.REV. 453 (1932).

Murchison, Brian C., *Speech and the Self-Realization Value*, 33 HARV. C.R.-C.L. L. REV. 443, 444 (1998).

NEMET-NEJAT, KAREN RHEA, DAILY LIFE IN ANCIENT MESOPOTAMIA (1998).

Nolan, Virginia E., & Edmund Ursin, *Dean Leon Green and Enterprise (No-Fault) Liability: Origins, Strategies, and Prospects*, 47 WAYNE L. REV. 91, 92-93 (2001).

Nolan, Virginia E., & Edmund Ursin, *The Deacademification of Tort Theory*, 48 U. KAN. L. REV. 59, 75-103 (1999).

O'Connell, Jeffery, Stephen J. Carroll, Michael Horowitz, Allan Abrahamse, and Alexander Karan, *Consumer Choice in the Minnesota Auto Insurance Market*, 24 WILLIAM & MARY L. REV. 825 (1998).

Owen, David G., *The Moral Foundations of Products Liability Law: Toward First Principles*, 68 NOTRE DAME L. REV. 427, 438-439 (1993).

Patterson, Dennis, *Normativity and Objectivity in Law*, 43 WILLIAM & MARY L.REV. 325, 328 (2001).

Pildes, Richard H., *Avoiding Balancing: The Role of Exclusionary Reasons in Constitutional Law*, 45 HASTINGS L.J. 711 (1994).

POLLOCK, FREDERICK, 2 HISTORY OF ENGLISH LAW 303-304 (1894).

POSNER, RICHARD A., ECONOMIC ANALYSIS OF LAW 36-37, 58, 59, 61, 64, 71, 80-81, 86, 99, 102, 118 (3d ed. 1986).

POSNER, RICHARD A., THE PROBLEMATICS OF MORAL AND LEGAL THEORY, reviewed in John Mikhail, *Law, Science, and Morality: A Review of Richard Posner's* THE PROBLEMATICS OF MORAL AND LEGAL THEORY, 54 STAN. L. REV. 1057, 1086-1087 (2002).

Posner, Richard A., *Wealth Maximization and Tort Law: A Philosophical Inquiry*, in DAVID G. OWEN, EDITOR, THE PHILOSOPHICAL FOUNDATIONS OF TORT LAW 99 (1995).

Post, Robert C., *Recuperating First Amendment Doctrine*, 47 STAN. L.REV. 1249 (1995).

Post, Robert C., *The Constitutional Concept of Public Discourse: Outrageous Opinion, Democratic Deliberation, and Hustler Magazine v. Falwell*, 103 HARV. L.REV. 601 (1990).

Post, Robert C., *The Management of Speech: Discretion and Rights*, 1984 SUP. CT. REV. 169, 193-206.

Post, Robert C., *Three Concepts of Privacy*, 89 GEO. L.J. 2087, 2097 (2001).

POSTGATE, J.N., EARLY MESOPOTAMIA; SOCIETY & ECONOMY AT THE DAWN OF HISTORY (1992).

Priest, George L., *Strict Products Liability: The Original Intent*, 10 CARDOZO L.REV. 2301, 2301 (1989).

PRITCHARD, JAMES B., ED., THE ANCIENT NEAR EAST – SUPPLEMENTARY TEXT AND PICTURES RELATING TO THE OLD TESTAMENT 87 (1969).

Prosser, William L., *Transferred Intent*, 45 TEX. L. REV. 650 (1967).

PUFENDORF, SAMUEL, ON THE DUTY OF MAN AND CITIZEN ACCORDING TO NATURAL LAW, Ch. II, Pt. 17 (1673) (Frank G. Moore, trans.).

Rabin, Robert L., *The Historical Development of the Fault Principle: A Reinterpretation*, 15 GA. L.REV. 925, 960-61 (1981).

Rachlinski, Jeffery J., *Misunderstanding Misability; Misallocating Responsibility*, 68 BROOKLYN L.REV. 1055, 1063N.24, 1091 (2003).

Redish, Martin H., *Self-Realization, Democracy, and Freedom of Expression: A Reply to Professor Baker*, 130 U. PA. L. REV. 678, 680 (1982).

Redish, Martin H., *The Value of Free Speech*, 130 U. PA. L. REV. 591 (1982).

Regan, Donald H., *The Supreme Court and State Protectionism: Making Sense of the Dormant Commerce Clause*, 84 MICH. L.REV. 1091, 1154 (1986).

Reynolds, Jr., Osborne M., *The Reasonable Man of Negligence Law: A Health Report on the "Odious Creature,"* 23 OKLA. L. REV. 410 (1970).

Richards, David A., *Free Speech and Obscenity Law: Toward a Moral Theory of the First Amendment*, 123 U. PA. L. REV. 45, 62 (1974).

ROBERTSON, DAVID W., WILLIAM POWERS JR., DAVID A. ANDERSON & OLIN GUY WELLBORN III, CASES AND MATERIALS ON TORTS 283 (3rd ed. 2004).

RORTY, RICHARD, CONTINGENCY, IRONY, AND SOLIDARITY 27-34 (1989).

Rosenblatt, Albert M., *The Fifty-Fifth Annual Cardozo Memorial Lecture: The Law's Evolution: Long Night's Journey into Day*, 24 CARDOZO L.REV. 2119, 2123-24 (2003).

ROST, H.T.D., THE GOLDEN RULE: A UNIVERSAL ETHIC 28, 39, 43, 49, 103, 114 (1986).

ROTH, MARTHA T., LAW COLLECTIONS FROM MESOPOTAMIA AND ASIA MINOR 13, 19 (2d ed. 1997).

Roux, Georges, *Did the Sumerians Emerge from the Sea?* in JEAN BOTTERO, ED., EVERYDAY LIFE IN ANCIENT MESOPOTAMIA 3 (2001) (English translation).

Rustad, Michael, & Thomas Koenig, *The Historical Continuity of Punitive Damages Awards*, 42 AM.U. L.REV. 1269 (1993).

SAGGS, H.W.F., EVERYDAY LIFE IN BABYLONIA & ASSYRIA (1965).

SALMOND, R. HEUSTON, ON THE LAW OF TORTS 9 (12th ed. 1957).

Geoffrey Sawyer, LAW IN SOCIETY 62 (1965).

Scallen, Eilleen A., *Evidence Law as Pragmatic Legal Rhetoric: Reconnecting Legal Scholarship, Teaching and Ethics*, 21 QLR 813, 834 (2003).

Scanlon, Thomas M., *A Theory of Freedom of Expression*, 1 PHIL. & PUB. AFF. 204, 213-24 (1972).

Schauer, Frederick, *Categories and the First Amendment: A Play in Three Acts*, 34 VANDERBILT L.REV. 265 (1981).

SCHAUER, FREDERICK, FREE SPEECH: A PHILOSOPHICAL ENQUIRY 6, 55, 56 (1982).

Schlag, Pierre, *The Problem of Transaction Costs*, 62 S. CAL. L.REV. 1661, 1661 (1989).

Schwab, Stewart J., *Coase Defends Coase: Why Lawyers Listen and Economists Do Not* (Book Review), 87 MICH. L.REV. 1171 (1989).

Schwartz, Gary, *Tort Law and the Economy in Nineteenth-Century American: A Reinterpretation*, 90 YALE L.J. 1717 (1981).

SCHWARTZ, MORTIMER D., RICHARD C. WYDICK, REX R. PERSCHBACHER, & DEBRA L. BASSETT, PROBLEMS IN LEGAL ETHICS 17-19 (5th ed. 2001).

Schwartz, Victor E., KATHRYN KELLY, & DAVID F. PARTLETT, PROSSER, WADE AND SCHWARTZ'S TORTS: CASES AND MATERIALS 2-3, 129-130 (10th ed. 2000).

Schwartz, Victor E., & Mark A. Behrens, *Federal Product Liability Reform in 1997: History and Public Policy Support Its Enactment Now*, 64 TENN. L.REV. 595, 597 (1997).

SHAFFERN, ROBERT W., LAW AND JUSTICE FROM ANTIQUITY TO ENLIGHTENMENT (Rowman and Littlefield Pubs. 2009).

Shapo, Marshall S., *In Search of the Law of Products Liability: The ALI Restatement Project*, 48 VAND.L.REV. 631, 698 (1995).

SHERMAN, CHARLES P., ED., EPITOME OF ROMAN LAW IN A SINGLE BOOK: A CONCISE COLLECTION OF ALMOST 700 SELECTED TEXTS OF PRINCIPLES AND RULES IN ROMAN JURISPRUDENCE 187, 191, 193, 207, 215 (1937).

SHERMAN, CHARLES P., I ROMAN LAW IN THE MODERN WORLD 11 (1917).

SHERMAN, CHARLES P., III ROMAN LAW IN THE MODERN WORLD 186-89 (1917).

Sherwin, Richard K., *Law's Beattitude: A Post-Nietzschean Account of Legitimacy*, 24 CARDOZO L.REV. 683, 692, 696 (2003).

Skelly, Mick, *The Definition of Care*, PHYSIOTHERAPY FRONTLINE, Oct. 2, 1996, at 2.

Silver, Theodore, *One Hundred Years of Harmful Error: The Historical Jurisprudence of Medical Malpractice*, 1992 WISC. L.REV. 1193, 1195.

SMOLLA, RODNEY A., JERRY FALWELL V LARRY FLYNT: THE FIRST AMENDMENT ON TRIAL (1988).

Special Committee on the Tort Liability System, *Towards a Jurisprudence of Injury: The Continuing Creation of a System of Substantive Justice in American Tort Law*, Committee's Preface 1-1, 14-1, 14-2 (1984).

Spieler, Emily A., *Perpetuating Risk? Workers' Compensation and the Persistence of Occupational Injuries*, 31 HOUS. L.REV. 119, 140-45 (1994).

Stockdale, Merren, & Philip J. Warelow, *Is the Complexity of Care a Paradox?*, 31 J. ADVANCED NURSING 1258, 1258-60, 1263 (2000).

STREET, THOMAS A., THE FOUNDATIONS OF LEGAL LIABILITY; VOL. I THEORY AND PRINCIPLES OF TORT vii, xi (1906).

Struve, Catherine T., *Doctors, the Adversary System, and Procedural Reform in Medical Liability Litigation*, 72 FORDHAM L.REV. 943, 976 (2004).

Sylvester, Douglas J., *Myth in Restorative Justice History*, 2003 UTAH L.REV. 471, 513.

TAYLOR, CHARLES, HUMAN AGENCY AND LANGUAGE, PHILOSOPHICAL PAPERS I (1986).

TAYLOR, CHARLES, SOURCES OF THE SELF, THE MAKING OF MODERN IDENTITY (1989).

TAYLOR, CHARLES, THE ETHICS OF AUTHENTICITY (1992).

Tracy, David, *The Hidden God: The Divine Other of Liberation*, 46 CROSS CURRENTS 1, 5 (1996).

UNGNAD, ARTHUR, SELECTED BABYLONIAN BUSINESS AND LEGAL DOCUMENTS OF THE HAMMURABI PERIOD (1907).

Van Alstyne, William M., *A Graphic Review of the Free Speech Clause*, 70 CAL. L.REV. 107 (1982).

Veenhof, Klaas R., *Before Hammurabi of Babylon: Law and the Laws in Early Mesopotamia*, in F.J.M. FEDBRUGGE, ED., THE LAW'S BEGINNINGS (2003).

VERSTEEG, RUSS, LAW IN THE ANCIENT WORLD §1.05, at 9 (2002).

VETRI, DOMINICK, LAWRENCE C. LEVINE, LUCINDA M. FINLEY, & JOAN E. VOGEL, TORT LAW AND PRACTICE 10-11 (2003).

WATSON, JEAN, NURSING: THE PHILOSOPHY AND SCIENCE OF CARING 8-10 (1979).

WEILER, PAUL C., A MEASURE OF MEDICAL MALPRACTICE: MEDICAL INJURY, MALPRACTICE LITIGATION, AND PATIENT COMPENSATION (1993).

Weingreen, J., *Concepts in Ancient Biblical Civil and Criminal Law*, THE IRISH JURIST 113, 123 (1989).

Wendel, W. Bradley, *Free Speech for Lawyers*, 28 Hastings Const. L.Q. 305, 422 (2001).

Wigmore, John H., *Responsibility for Tortious Acts: Its History*, 7 HARV. L.REV. 315, *316*, 383, 441 (1894).

WINFIELD, PERCY H., THE CHIEF SOURCES OF LEGAL HISTORY 22-23, 51 (1925).

Winfield, Percy H., *The History of Negligence in the Law of Torts*, 42 L.Q.REV. 184, 192-93, *195*, 199 (1926).

Wright, R. George, *Hustler Magazine v. Falwell and the Role of the First Amendment*, 19 CUMB. L.REV. 19 (1988/1989).

Wright, Richard W., *Right, Justice and Tort Law*, in DAVID G. OWEN, EDITOR, THE PHILOSOPHICAL FOUNDATIONS OF TORT LAW 159 (1995).

Woodbine, *The Origin of the Action of Trespass*, 33 YALE L.J. 799 (1923), 34 Yale L.J. 343 (1934).

Yaron, Reuven, *The Goring Ox in Near Eastern Laws*, in HAIM H. COHN, ED., JEWISH LAW IN ANCIENT AND MODERN ISRAEL 50 (1971).

Yaron, Ruben, The Laws of Eshnunna 23 (1969).

Studies, Statistics, Statutes, and Restatements:

BUREAU OF JUSTICE STATISTICS BULLETIN 1 (Sept. 1999).

FL. CODE §766.301-316.

IDAHO CODE § 6-904B (Michie Supp. 2003).

MICH. COMP. LAWS ANN. § 600.2591(1) (West 2000).

MICH. COMP. LAWS ANN. §600.2946 (West 2000).

NATIONAL SAFETY COUNCIL, INJURY FACTS 83 (1999)).

RESTATEMENT (FIRST) OF TORTS § 14 cmt. a (1934).

RESTATEMENT (FIRST) OF TORTS §761 (1965).

RESTATEMENT (SECOND) OF TORTS § 2 cmt. a (1965).

RESTATEMENT (SECOND) OF TORTS § 222A (2000).

RESTATEMENT (SECOND) OF TORTS § 229 (2000).

RESTATEMENT (SECOND) OF TORTS § 281 (2000).

RESTATEMENT (SECOND) OF TORTS § 283 (1965).

RESTATEMENT (SECOND) OF TORTS § 283 cmt. b (1965).

RESTATEMENT (SECOND) OF TORTS § 288A (1965).

RESTATEMENT (SECOND) OF TORTS §§ 289(a), *(b)* (1965).

RESTATEMENT (SECOND) OF TORTS § 291 (1965).

RESTATEMENT (SECOND) OF TORTS § 293(a) (1965).

RESTATEMENT (SECOND) OF TORTS § 296(1) (1965).

RESTATEMENT (SECOND) OF TORTS § 299A (1965).

RESTATEMENT (SECOND) OF TORTS §§ 314A & 314B (1965).

RESTATEMENT (SECOND) OF TORTS § 343(a) (1965).

RESTATEMENT (SECOND) OF TORTS § 388 (1965).

RESTATEMENT (SECOND) OF TORTS § 402A (1965).

RESTATEMENT (SECOND) OF TORTS § 402A cmts. k, m (1965).

RESTATEMENT (SECOND) OF TORTS § 435(1) (1965).

RESTATEMENT (SECOND) OF TORTS § 466 (1965).

RESTATEMENT (SECOND) OF TORTS §§ 496F-496G (1965 & Supp. 2004).

RESTATEMENT (SECOND) OF TORTS § 500 cmt. A (1965).

RESTATEMENT (SECOND) OF TORTS §519(1) (1977).

RESTATEMENT (SECOND) OF TORTS § 520(f) (1977).

RESTATEMENT (SECOND) OF TORTS § 525 (2000).

RESTATEMENT (SECOND) OF TORTS § 526 (2000).

RESTATEMENT (SECOND) OF TORTS § 530 (2000).

RESTATEMENT (SECOND) OF TORTS § 538 (1977).

RESTATEMENT (SECOND) OF TORTS §541 (1965).

RESTATEMENT (SECOND) OF TORTS § 558 (2000).

RESTATEMENT (SECOND) OF TORTS §652E (1965).

RESTATEMENT (SECOND) OF TORTS § 652H (1976).

RESTATEMENT (SECOND) OF TORTS § 885 (1979).

RESTATEMENT (SECOND) OF TORTS § 874 (1977).

RESTATEMENT (SECOND) OF TORTS § 924(b) (1979).

RESTATEMENT (SECOND) OF TORTS § 924(c) (1979).

RESTATEMENT (THIRD) OF TORTS: APPORTIONMENT OF LIAB. § 25 (2000).

RESTATEMENT (THIRD) OF TORTS: APPORTIONMENT OF LIAB. § 26 (2000).

RESTATEMENT (THIRD) OF TORTS: LIAB. FOR PHYSICAL HARM § 3 cmt. l (Tentative Draft No. 1, 2001).

RESTATEMENT (THIRD) OF TORTS: LIAB. FOR PHYSICAL HARM § 12 (Tentative Draft No. 1, 2001).

RESTATEMENT (THIRD) OF TORTS: LIAB. FOR PHYSICAL HARM § 12 cmt. c. (Tentative Draft No. 1, 2001).

RESTATEMENT (THIRD) OF TORTS: PRODUCTS LIAB. § 1 cmt. C, n.1 (1998).

RESTATEMENT (THIRD) OF TORTS: PRODUCTS LIAB. § 2(b) (1998).

RESTATEMENT (THIRD) OF TORTS: PRODUCTS LIAB. § 2 cmt. d (1998).

RESTATEMENT (THIRD) OF TORTS: PRODUCTS LIAB. § 8 (1998) (tentative draft).
29 USC §653(b)(4).
UTAH CODE ANN. §78-27-42 (2002).
VA. CODE. ANN. §§38.2-5000 to 5021.

Cases, Statutes, and Other Authority:

Abb v. N. Pac. R.R. Co., 68 P. 954 (Wash. 1902).
Abercrombie v. Carpenter, 43 So. 746, 747 (Ala. 1907).
Abood v Detroit Bd. of Educ., 431 U.S. 209, 231 (1977).
Abrams v United States, 250 U.S. 616, 630 (1919) (Holmes, J., dissenting).
Aisole v. Dean, 574 So.2d 1248, 1253-54 (La. 1991).
Akers v Alvey, 338 F.3d 491 (6th Cir. 2003).
Albergo v Hellenic Lines, Inc., 658 F.2d 66, 70 (2nd Cir. 1981).
American Export Lines, Inc. v. Alvez, 446 U.S. 274, 284 (1980).
American States Ins. Co. v. Audubon Country Club, 650 S.W.2d 252 (Ky. 1983).
Anderson v. Oklahoma Temp. Svcs., Inc., 925 P.2d 574, 576 (Okla. Civ. App. 1996).
Arkansas Valley Elec. Coop. Corp. v. Davis, 800 S.W.2d 420, 423 (Ark. 1990).
Aves v. Shah, 997 F.2d 762, 765 (10th Cir. 1993).
Ballew v. Aiello, 422 S.W.2d 396, 399 (Mo. Ct. App. 1967).
Baxter v Ford Motor Co., 12 P.2d 409 (Wash. 1932).
Beech v. Outboard Marine Corp., 584 So.2d 447, 450 (Ala. 1991).
Bierczynski v Rogers, 239 A.2d 219 (Del. 1968).
Bose Corp. v Consumers Union of United States, Inc., 466 U.S. 485, 503-504 (1984).
Bowers v. Sprouse, 492 S.E.2d 637 (Va. 1997).
Boyce v. Brown, 77 P.2d 455, 458 (Ariz. 1938).
Bradley v. Appalachian Power Co., 256 S.E.2d 879, 889 (W. Va. 1979).
Brown v Board of Education, 347 U.S. 483 (1954).
Canterbury v. Spence, 464 F.2d 772, 780 (D.C. Cir. 1972).
Carlson v. Green, 446 U.S. 14, 17-23 (1980).
Campuzano v. Islamic Republic of Iran, 281 F.Supp.2d 258, 279 (D. D.C. 2003).
Carey v Population Services Intl., 431 U.S. 678 (1977).
Carnes v. Thompasin, 48 S.W.2d 903, 904 (Mo. 1932).
Centman v. Cobb, 581 N.E.2d 1286, 1288 (Ind. Ct. App. 1991).
Champion v. Gray, 478 So. 2d 17, 18-19 (Fla. 1985).
Chaplinsky v New Hampshire, 315 U.S. 568, 571-72 (1942).

Clinkscales v Carver, 136 P.2d 777 (Ca. 1943).

Cohen v Petty, 65 F.2d 820 (D.C. Cir. 1933).

Coker v Georgia, 433 U.S. 584, 597 (1977).

Colonial Inn Motor Lodge v. Gay, 680 N.E.2d 407, 416 (Ill. App. Ct. 1997).

Commercial Business Systems, Inc. v Bellsouth Services, Inc., 453 N.E.2d 261 (Va. 1995).

Commonwealth v Hall, 830 A.2d 537, 544 (Pa. Sup. Ct. 2003).

Consolidated Edison Co. v Public Service Commn., 447 U.S. 530, 534n.2 (1980).

Consolidated Rail Corp. v. Gottshall, 512 U.S. 532, 542-43 (1994).

Conway v O'Brien, 111 F.2d 611, 612 (2nd Cir. 1940), rev'd, 312 U.S. 492 (1941).

Cook & Nichol, Inc. v. Plimsoll Club, 451 F.2d 505, 509 (5th Cir. 1971).

Cox v. Louisiana, 379 U.S. 536, 555 (1965).

Cusseaux v. Pickett, 652 A.2d 789, 794 (N.J. Super. Ct. Law Div. 1994).

Davidson v. Reed, 337 So.2d 1288, 1290 (Ala. 1976).

Daley v. LaCroix, 179 N.W.2d 390, 395 (Mich. 1970).

Doe v Hartz, 52 F.Supp.2d 1027 (N.D. Iowa 1999).

Doe v Johnson, 817 F.Supp. 1382 (W.D. Mich. 1993).

Donnell v. California Western School of Law, 200 Cal.App.3d 715, 728, 246 Cal.Rptr. 199, 207 (Cal. Ct. App. 1988).

Duffey Law Office v. Tank Transport, Inc., 535 N.W.2d 91, 96 (Wis. Ct. App. 1995).

Dun & Bradstreet, Inc. v Greenmoss Builders, Inc., 472 U.S. 749, 757-58 (1985).

Dworkin v. Hustler Magazine Inc., 867 F.2d 1188, 1190 (9th Cir. 1989).

Eisenstadt v Baird, 405 U.S. 438 (1972).

Enright v Eli Lilly & Co., 77 N.Y.2d 377, 570 N.E.2d 198, 568 N.Y.S.2d 550 (N.Y. Ct. App. 1991).

Estate of Sinthasomphone v. City of Milwaukee, 785 F. Supp 1343, 1349 (E.D. Wis. 1992).

Estate of Williams v. Vandeberg, 620 N.W.2d 187, 191 (S.D. 2000).

Examining Bd. Of Engineers, Architects & Surveyors v Flores de Otero, 426 U.S. 572, 605-606 (1976).

F.W. Woolworth v Kirby, 302 So. 67, 71 (Ala. Sup. Ct. 1974).

FCC v Pacifica Foundation, 438 U.S. 726, 747 (1978).

Federal Deposit Ins. Corp. v. Dannen, 747 F. Supp. 1357, 1362 (W.D. Mo. 1990).

Feltmeier v. Feltmeier, 798 N.E.2d 75, 87 (Ill. 2003).

Ferrie v D'Arc, 155 A.2d 257 (N.J. 1959), reversing, 150 A.2d 83 (N.J. Super. Ct. 1959).

Garratt v. Dailey, 279 P.2d 1091, 1094 (Wash. 1955).

Gertz v. Robert Welch, Inc., 418 U.S. 323, 345 (1974).

Gess v. United States, 991 F. Supp. 1332, 1347 (M.D. Ala. 1997).

Ghaffari v Turner Constr. Co., 676 NW2d 259 (Mich. Ct. App. 2003).

Grant v. Reader's Digest Ass'n, Inc., 151 F.2d 733, 734 (2nd Cir. 1945).

Gregory v. Cincinnati, Inc., 538 N.W.2d 325, 326 (Mich. 1995).

Griswold v Connecticut, 381 U.S. 479 (1965).

Gryc v. Dayton-Hudson Corp., 297 N.W.2d 727, 741 (Minn. 1980).

Hamilton v. Beretta, U.S.A., Corp., 96 N.Y.2d 222, 727 N.Y.S.2d 7, 750 N.E.2d 1055, 1061 (N.Y. Ct. App. 2001).

Harper & Row Publishers, Inc. v. Nation Enters., 471 U.S. 539, 559 (1985).

Harris v. Pennsylvania R.R. Co., 50 F.2d 866, 868 (4th Cir. 1931).

Head & Seemann, Inc. v. Gregg, 311 N.W.2d 667, 671 (Wis. Ct. App. 1981).

Heath v. Swift Wings, Inc., 252 S.E.2d 526, 529(N.C. Ct. App. 1979).

Henningsen v Bloomfield Motors Co., 161 A.2d 69 (N.J. 1960).

Hodges v. Jewel Cos., 390 N.E.2d 930 (Ill. App. Ct. 1979).

House v. Kellerman, 519 S.W.2d 380, 383 (Ky. Ct. App. 1974).

Howard v University of Medicine and Dentistry of New Jersey, 800 A.2d 73, 83-84 (N.J. 2002).

Howlett v. Birkdale Shipping Co., S.A., 512 U.S. 92 (1994).

Hurley v Irish-American Gay, Lesbian and Bisexual Group, 515 U.S. 557, 573 (1996).

Hurt v. Freeland, 589 N.W.2d 551, 555 (N.D. 1999).

Hustler Magazine v Falwell, 485 U.S. 46 (1988).

In re Tutorship of Witt, 747 So.2d 1142, 1150 (La. Ct. App. 1999).

Indiana Harbor Belt R.R. Co. v American Cyanamid Co., 916 F.2d 1174 (7th Cir. 1990).

Ingram v. Nationwide Mut. Ins. Co., 129 S.E.2d 222, 225 (N.C. 1963).

Janelsins v. Button, 648 A.2d 1039 (Md. Ct. Spec. App. 1994).

Johnson v. Univ. Health Servs., Inc., 161 F.3d 1334, 1341 (11th Cir. 1998).

Jones v. Barwick, 386 So. 2d 7, 8 (Fla. Dist. Ct. App. 1980).

Jones v. Clinton, 990 F. Supp. 657, 677 (E.D. Ark. 1998).

Kitsap County Transp. Co. v. Harvey, 15 F.2d 166 (9th Cir. 1926).

LaCava v. New Orleans, 159 So. 2d 362 (La. Ct. App. 1964).

Lacy v. G.D. Searle & Co., 567 A.2d 398 (Del.. 1989).

Lawrence v Texas, 539 U.S. 558 (2003).

Lawson v. Murray, 515 U.S. 1110, 1111-13(1995).

Liberty Lobby, Inc. v Anderson, 746 F.2d 1563, 1568 (D.C. Cir. 1984), *vacated on other grounds*, Anderson v Liberty Lobby, Inc., 477 U.S. 242 (1986).

Lockhart v. List, 665 A.2d 1176, 1182 (Pa. 1995).

Lopez v. Surchia, 246 P.2d 111, 113 (Cal. Ct. App. 1952).

Loveday v Travelers Ins. Co., 585 So.2d 597, 602 (La. Ct. App. 1991).

MacPherson v Buick Motor Co., 111 NE 1050 (N.Y. 1916).

Mahan v. State, 191 A. 575 (Md. 1937).

Mahnke v. Moore, 77 A.2d 923, 926 (Md. 1951).

Maryland Cas. Co. v. Delzer, 283 N.W.2d 244, 248 (S.D. 1979).

Mastland, Inc. v. Evans Furniture, Inc., 498 N.W.2d 682 (Iowa 1993).

Matter of Sloat v. Board of Examiners, 9 N.E.2d 12, 15 (N.Y. 1937)).

Marbury v. Madison, 5 U.S. 137, 176 (1803).

McCulloch v. Maryland, 17 U.S. 316, 421 (1819).

McGuire v. Almy, 8 N.E.2d 760 (Mass. 1937).

Miamisburg Train Derailment Litig., 725 N.E.2d 738, 746 (Ohio Ct. App. 1999).

Michael & Philip, Inc. v Sierra, 776 So.2d 294, 297-298 (Fla. Ct. App. 2000).

Milkovich v Lorain Journal Co., 497 U.S. 1, 22 (1990).

Molzof v. United States, 502 U.S. 301, 312 (1992).

Moore v. Capital Transit Co., 226 F.2d 57 (D.C. Cir. 1955), *cert. denied*, 350 U.S. 966 (1956).

Morel v. Franklin Stores Corp., 91 So. 2d 42, 44 (La. Ct. App. 1957).

NAACP v. Claiborne Hardware Co., 458 U.S. 886, 916 (1982).

Natrona County v. Blake, 81 P.3d 948, 951 (Wyo. 2003).

Neiman-Marcus v Lait, 13 F.R.D. 311 (S.D. N.Y. 1952).

New York Times Co. v Sullivan, 376 U.S. 254, 270 (1964).

O'Brien v. Muskin Corp., 463 A.2d 298, 306 (N.J. 1983).

Otterbeck v. Lamb, 456 P.2d 855 (Nev. 1969).

Parlato v. Equitable Life Assurance Soc'y, 749 N.Y.S.2d. 216, 223 (N.Y. App. Div. 2002), *leave denied*, 787 N.E.2d 1164 (N.Y. 2003).

Patin v. State Farm Ins. Co., 395 So. 2d 466, 469 (La. Ct. App. 1981).

Patton v. Hutchinson Wil-Rich Mfg. Co., 861 P.2d 1299, 1303-04 (Kan. 1993).

Paul v Davis, 424 U.S. 693, 723 (1976).

Pavlik v. Kornhaber, 761 N.E.2d 175, 187 (Ill. App. Ct. 2001).

Pierson v. Ray, 386 U.S. 547, 554 (1967).

Planned Parenthood of Southeastern Pa. v. Casey, 505 U.S. 833, 850 (1992).

Prentis v. Yale Mfg. Co., 365 N.W.2d 176, 186 (Mich. 1984).

Price v. Kitsap Transit, 886 P.2d 556 (Wash. 1994).

Procunier v. Martinez, 416 U.S. 396, 427-428 (1974).

Pullen v. Novak, 99 N.W.2d 16, 25 (Neb. 1959).

Redford v. City of Seattle, 615 P.2d 1285, 1289 (Wash. 1980).

Reed v. Maley, 74 S.W. 1079, 1080 (Ky. 1903).

Renko v. McLean, 697 A.2d 468, 472 (Md. 1997).

Rentz v. Brown, 464 S.E.2d 617 (Ga. Ct. App. 1995).

Riss v New York, 240 N.E.2d 860 (N.Y. Ct. App. 1968).

Roberts v. State, 396 So. 2d 566 (La. Ct. App. 1981).

Roberts v. United States Jaycees, 468 U.S. 609, 628 (1984).
Roe v Wade, 410 U.S. 113 (1973).
Rosenblatt v Baer, 383 US 75, 86 (1966).
Rosenbloom v. Metromedia, Inc., 403 U.S. 29, 78 (1971).
Rouleau v. Blotner, 152 A. 916, 916 (N.H. 1931).
Saret-Cook v. Gilbert, Kelly, Crowley & Jennett, 88 Cal. Rptr.2d. 732, 746 (Cal. Ct. App. 1999).
Seeholzer v. Kellstone, Inc., 610 N.E.2d 594, 597 (Ohio Ct. App. 1992).
Singleton v. Northfield Ins. Co., 826 So.2d 55, 69 (La. Ct. App. 2002).
Smith v. Van Gorkom, 488 A.2d 858, 872 (Del. 1985).
Smith v. Walter C. Best, Inc., 927 F.2d. 736, 741-42 (3d Cir. 1990).
Spano v. Perini Corp., 250 N.E.2d 31, 34 (N.Y. 1969).
Spence v Washington, 418 U.S. 405, 410-11 (1974).
Spivey v. Battaglia, 258 So. 2d 815, 817 (Fla. 1972).
Standard v. Hobbs, 589 S.E.2d 634, 638-39 (Ga. Ct. App. 2003).
Stitt v. Holland Abundant Life Fellowship, 462 Mich. 591, 614 N.W.2d 88 (2000).
Storjohn v. Fay, 519 N.W.2d 521 (Neb. 1994).
Tauber-Arons Auctioneer Co. v. Superior Court, 161 Cal.Rptr. 789, 794-95 (Cal. Ct. App 1980).
Tenney v. Brandhove, 341 U.S. 367, 377 (1951).
The Florida Star v B.J.F., 491 U.S. 524, 553 (1989).
The Max Morris, 137 U.S. 1, 14-15 (1890).
Time, Inc. v. Firestone, 424 U.S. 448, 471 (1976).
Time, Inc. v. Hill, 385 U.S. 374, 414n.5 (1967).
Tobia v. Cooper Hosp. Univ. Med. Ctr., 643 A.2d 1 (N.J. 1994).
Twyman v. Twyman, 855 S.W.2d 619, 621-22 (Tex. 1993).
United States v Associated Press, 52 F. Supp. 362, 372 (S.D. N.Y. 1943).
United States v. Burke, 504 U.S. 229, 234-35 (1992).
United States v Carroll Towing Co., 159 F.2d 169 (2nd Cir. 1947).
United States v Kubrick 444 U.S. 111, 124 (1979).
United States v. O'Brien, 391 U.S. 367, 376 (1968).
United States v National Treasury Employees, 513 U.S. 454, 464 (1995).
Vaillancourt v. Med. Ctr. Hosp., Inc., 425 A.2d 92, 93 (Vt. 1980).
Varelis v. Northwestern Mem. Hosp., 657 N.E.2d 997, 1004 (Ill. 1995).
Virginia v Black, 538 U.S. 343 (2003).
Volk v. Baldazo, 651 P.2d 11, 12 (Idaho 1982).
Voss v. Black & Decker Mfg. Co., 450 N.E.2d 204, 210 (N.Y. 1983).
Wal-Mart Discount City v Meyers, 738 S.W.2d 841 (Ky. Ct. App. 1987).
Walta v. Gallegos Law Firm, P.C., 40 P.3d 449, 460 (N.M. Ct. App. 2001).
Whitney v. California, 274 U.S. 357, 375 (1927).
Wisconsin v Mitchell, 508 U.S. 476 (1993).

Woodall v. Castner-Knott Dry Goods Co., 673 So.2d 769 (Ala. Ct. App. 1995).

Ybarra v. Spangard, 154 P.2d 687, 689 (Cal. 1944).

Acknowledgments

I first acknowledge the privilege of employment at Western Michigan University Cooley Law School allowing me to serve students, faculty, and staff, and to draw from them inspiration and support for this and other scholarship. The time, capability, and purpose to write, and especially to write about law and history, are each graces bestowed by the university and law school. Western Michigan University is a Carnegie Foundation research university with high research activity, one of only 76 such public universities in the nation and one of only 90 universities with both law and medical schools. Western Michigan University Cooley Law School is rated among the top of over 200 law schools in the nation as to practical training, diversity, and graduate programs.

I particularly acknowledge the university's President Dr. John Dunn, law school's President and Dean Don LeDuc, and law faculty colleagues teaching and writing in my field Paul Sorensen, Mark Dotson, Monica Nuckolls, Linda Kisabeth, Chris Trudeau, Chris Hastings, and Lauren Rousseau. These professors each practiced law before coming to teaching, meaning that they know of that which they write and speak. I also thank head librarian Aletha Honsowitz and reference librarian Amy Ash for research assistance.

I also acknowledge and thank Western Michigan University Cooley Law School students Desiree Benedict, Erick Bradtke, Thomas Irvine, Cedelle Kupfer-Escobedo, Alex Penny, Mary Redford, Abigail Savin, Millicent Southern, Wendy Swierbut, Shaydon Weaver, and Natalie Winquist for edit and proofread of the manuscript. Law students in their curiosity and ambitions were inspiration for this book. Law students know that law practice is a ministry of justice, as Justice Thomas McIntyre Cooley wrote. Things will be alright if law scholars and practitioners, and others who influence tort law, keep tort practice that way.

I also acknowledge the work of student editors of the Louisiana Law Review, New England Law Review, Thomas M. Cooley Law Review, University of Detroit-Mercy Law Review, and Whittier Law Review, and professional editors of the ABA Tort Trial & Insurance Practice Law Journal and Michigan Bar Journal, on articles from which I drew or after which I patterned above chapters. This book's style is for readability, omitting footnotes and citations. Readers should be able to identify quoted sources from the text and locate their citations in the bibliography. If not, then I have heavily footnoted versions of each chapter with those specific citations to volume and page number from which I can provide readers with sources.

About the Author

Nelson Miller is professor and associate dean at Western Michigan University Thomas M. Cooley Law School. Before joining WMU-Cooley, Dean Miller practiced civil litigation for 16 years, representing individuals, corporations, agencies, and public and private universities. He has published 24 books and dozens of book chapters and articles on law and law practice. The State Bar of Michigan recognized Dean Miller with the John W. Cummiskey Award for pro-bono service. He earned his law degree at the University of Michigan while working for the law firm that later became Fajen and Miller, PLLC, where after nearly 30 years he remains of counsel. Harvard University Press included Dean Miller among 26 law professors featured in its book *What the Best Law Teachers Do*.